The Hertfordshire Village Book

Other counties in this series include:

Avon*	Middlesex*
Bedfordshire*	Norfolk*
Berkshire*	Northamptonshire*
Buckinghamshire*	Nottinghamshire*
Cambridgeshire*	Oxfordshire*
Cheshire*	Powys Montgomery*
Devon*	Shropshire*
Dorset	Somerset*
Essex*	Staffordshire*
Gloucestershire*	Suffolk
Hampshire*	Surrey
Herefordshire*	East Sussex
Kent	West Sussex
Lancashire*	Warwickshire*
Leicestershire & Rutland*	West Midlands*
Lincolnshire*	Wiltshire
	Worcestershire*

*Published in conjunction with County Federations of Women's Institutes

The Hertfordshire Village Book

Compiled by the Hertfordshire
Federation of Women's Institutes from notes
and illustrations sent by Institutes in the County

Published jointly by
Countryside Books, Newbury
and the HFWI, St Albans

First Published 1986
Reprinted 1990
© Hertfordshire Federation of Women's Institutes 1986

Countryside Books
3 Catherine Road
Newbury, Berkshire

ISBN 0 905392 71 X

Cover Photograph is of Westmill

Produced through MRM Associates Ltd, Reading
Printed in England by Borcombe Printers, Reading

Foreword

Although Hertfordshire is one of England's smaller counties, it is one of great contrast, from the south, with its sprawling extension of London's suburbs, to the north, where narrow lanes crisscross the mainly unspoilt countryside dotted with out of the way villages.

Ever since the Romans built Watling Street (A5) and Ermine Street (A10) Hertfordshire has been a county sliced by roads and now by modern motorways, the M1 and M25. Travellers have tended to pass through this county which is so rich in history, enroute to the north or south, so hopefully this book will persuade them to stop, explore and enjoy.

In order to produce the book many people have delved deep to find an amazing amount of detail and local knowledge. Delightful village tales have been remembered, not only by WI members, but where no WI was present, kind friends have been approached so as to give complete coverage of the county. It will be found that some articles are from contributors from outside the county boundary, since after the re-alignment of this imaginary line some WIs, who were beyond the margin, chose to remain within the Hertfordshire Federation, and so of course they are included.

We have had enormous pleasure in collecting material for this book and are most grateful to all the contributors, with apologies to those whose efforts have not been included through lack of space. You will find as you read that there is no such place as an uninteresting village, especially to those who live there, and we as WI members with our roots in rural areas do all we can to preserve the history of our villages.

Ann Roxburgh
County Chairman

The County of Hertfordshire

St. Albans Abbey

LETCHWO

HITCHIN

HARPENDEN

M.1.

HEMEL
HEMPSTEAD

ST. ALBANS

M.10

M.25

WATFORD

RICKMANSWORTH

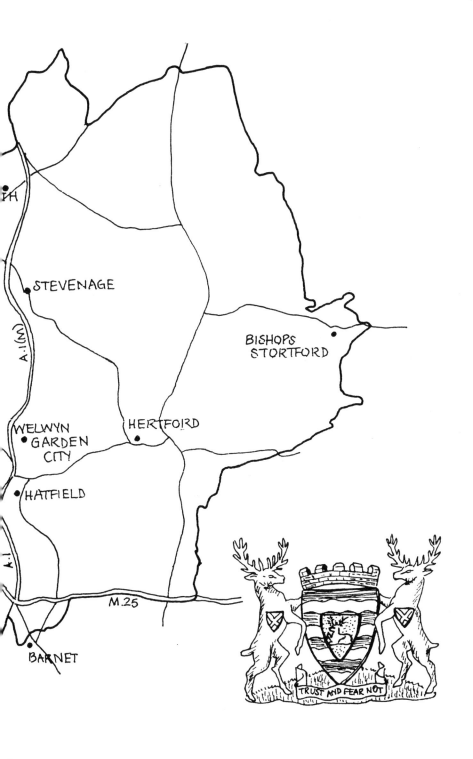

IH

STEVENAGE

A.1(M)

A.1

BISHOPS
STORTFORD

WELWYN
GARDEN
CITY

HERTFORD

HATFIELD

M.25

BARNET

TRUST AND FEAR NOT

Acknowledgements

The HFWI would like to thank all those members and their Institutes who have worked so hard to research and provide information and drawings for their villages. Also a special thank you to Heather Harris, co-ordinator for the project.

Our thanks are also due to the following for assistance in providing material:

Audrey Barry (drawing of the Hertfordshire hart)
Jean Davis (Aldbury)
Tom Doig (Barkway)
Tony Gardner (Bayford & Brickendon)
Joan Hands (Bourne End & Boxmoor)
Heather Harris (line map of the county)
Edna Holden (Standon & Puckeridge)
Bertha Kilbey (Bramfield)
David Robertson (Aldenham)
A. J. Ward (Nash Mills)

Abbots Langley 🦢

The Domesday Book describes Abbots Langley as the Langlai (long lea) belonging to the Abbot of St. Albans. It was a district of meadows and woods stretching north along the ridge of the hill and west down to the river Gade where there were two mills. There was mentioned a resident priest, a knight and about nineteen village men and their families.

The Langley Abbot continued to belong to the Abbey of St. Albans until the time of the Dissolution by Henry VIII and its history is therefore in the records of the Abbey. For instance in 1349 it is recorded that 79 people from the parish died from the Black Death.

Two centuries earlier, Nicholas Breakspear, the only English Pope was born in the district and would have attended the church as a boy. Failing to become a Monk at St. Albans Abbey, he succeeded when he went to France and later on to Rome where he became Pope Adrian IV (1154–59).

The *Guinness Book of Records* mentions Abbots Langley as the home of Elizabeth Greenhill who in the 17th century mothered thirty nine children (thirty two daughters and seven sons) all of whom survived to adulthood; the youngest son Thomas becoming a surgeon.

Today these estates and some of the farm land are covered with modern houses of many styles, making Abbots Langley a pleasant place in which to live. The modern village still stands at the top of the hill where the church has stood for nearly 1000 years. It is now flanked by a new library building, where the church school used to stand, and opposite is St. Saviours, a Roman Catholic Church.

Further down the High Street, past the old cottages and the shops new and old, is the Methodist Church and one of the halls run by the Parish Council. Nearby is a busy Doctor's Surgery.

Beyond this and further down the hill is Kitters Green, once a separate hamlet, complete with cottages, a pond and its own village pound, still a green space where people can sit and admire the playing fields opposite in the grounds of the now vanished manor house. There are cricket and football pitches and tennis courts as well as children's swings and slides near the sports and social centre.

The old school has been replaced by a modern building set further back from the road. On the other side of the village there is a second primary school near a few shops, a hall and the Baptist

Church. There is a Catholic primary school and recently the village welcomed Breakspear School for Handicapped children.

Aldbury

People have been coming to Aldbury for a very long time.

Bronze Age men were buried here. Iron Age men, with primitive implements and much hard labour, made dykes near the northwest boundary of the parish and settled for a while on the high common near Ashridge. Belgic men were cremated here shortly before the Romans came and a Roman road is alleged to have passed by the spot where the Valiant Trooper now stands. When Saxons made their home here in the 8th or 9th century, they called it 'Aldeberie' meaning 'old fortified place'. But no one now knows where the fortifications were.

Nowadays the visitors come. Bus-loads of over-60s hurry in for their teas at Town Farm. Straggles of school-children, clipboards at the ready, are marshalled to inspect the old houses, the green, the church or the stocks and whipping post by the pond. Cyclists stack up their machines outside the Greyhound before attempting the long pull up Toms Hill, once known as the Holloway.

One of the favourite places is the monument to the 3rd Duke of Bridgewater who lived at Ashridge, which stands high on the hillside overlooking the village. 'The Canal Duke', they called him; the 'Father of Inland Navigation'. But his most famous canal was far away to the north and he had nothing to do with the building of the Grand Union Canal (once the Grand Junction) which runs through the parish. In late Victorian times, wagonettes of children on Sunday School outings would make for the Monument for their picnics, and children from Aldbury would earn a penny or two for minding the horses.

They were still making straw plait in the village then, though the bottom had dropped out of the market with the import of oriental plaits. In the early part of the 19th century women, children and even men earned good money plaiting for the straw hat makers in Luton. Each Friday a procession of plaiters, their wares wrapped carefully in a clean cloth, made their way to Tring market to sell to the dealers. Village children learned to plait from the age of four, and plait schools were held in several of the cottages.

One of the few occasions when Aldbury made news in the national papers was in 1891. Poachers near the Stocks estate were surprised by two gamekeepers. A fight took place and the game-keepers were murdered after a violent struggle. The death sentence passed on two of the three poachers provoked a leading article in the *Times* on the day of execution, 18th March, 1892, and it was also debated in the House of Commons. Afterwards children in the village were terrified to pass the wood 'because they used to say the ghosts walked'.

Aldbury people who were born here or who came before the last war tell of the changes in their lifetime. In the 1930s almost all the cottages were tenanted, as were most of the houses except the rectory and two other large properties. These three had indoor sanitation, but it was an earth closet across the yard for the servants there, and down the garden for the cottage dwellers. Electricity reached the village in 1929, but it was 1976 before Aldbury had main sewerage.

As elderly tenants have left or died, their cottages have been sold. When the Ashridge Estate broke up at the end of the 1920s, cottage tenants were offered their homes for a price of £50 each; now the asking price for one of these terraced cottages is over £70,000 – an astronomic rise of 145,000%! Prices such as these force children from village families to go elsewhere when they want a home of their own, or to rent a council house when one is available. Some council houses have been bought, so the next generation will be better placed.

Aldbury is an old village, but it is not a fossilised village. Its community is continually changing though luckily there are still families here whose ancestors came two hundred years ago or more. We hope that it will remain what it is now – a living village.

Aldenham

Aldenham certainly dates from Saxon times and it is believed that the chancel of the Church of St. John the Baptist is the site of a Saxon church built by King Offa, King of Mercia (785 AD). In the Treasury of Westminster Abbey is a charter, which is the earliest they possess, in which lands were granted at Aldenham in return for the present of a gold armlet.

The Domesday Book of 1086 has this entry with regard to Aldenham – 'Eldeham: Westminster Abbey before and after 1066: Geoffrey de Bec from St. Albans Church'. Letchmore Heath is not listed in the Domesday Book and the first reference to any of its inhabitants was in the 16th century. But the name Letchmore originates from the Anglo Saxon words 'Leche mere' meaning 'dirty pond'. The pond is still there and a very beautiful feature of the village – but it is not dirty!

The Parish of Aldenham, which contains the minute village of Aldenham and the village of Letchmore Heath, has a population of about 2,500.

Today the Parish is threatened by the expansion of London to the north west. Marble Arch is only 14 miles away; the M1 cuts through the western boundary of the parish and the final piece of the M25 lies to the north. The Parish of Aldenham is thus a 'green lung' preserved by being in the Green Belt, and Aldenham and Letchmore Heath are both conservation areas. A Country Park has been constructed at Aldenham Old Reservoir and a nature reserve at the New Reservoir. The parish is much visited in the summer by Londoners who may wish to visit the country and Letchmore Heath with its 17th century inn, picturesque village green and pond, and its many 16th century cottages. The 12th century Aldenham Church is a beautiful building, with many fine brasses and tombs, with a fine peal of bells. The church is unique as its tower and tower buttresses have been built using Hertfordshire puddingstone, a very rare geological rock found only around the area of Aldenham and Radlett.

The inhabitants of the parish have changed dramatically in the last 60 years. In 1920 Letchmore Heath was an isolated village which the residents rarely had to leave, as all that was necessary was available within the village itself. There were then three pubs, two village stores – one with a Post Office; a baker; a butcher; an undertaker; a haberdashery and two tailors. A shepherd lived in Jasmin Cottage and he kept his sheep on what is now the Aldenham School playing fields.

There was a village school, two chapels and 90% of the residents worked on the local farm, Aldenham House or Aldenham School. In 1986 there is only one pub and a Krishna Shop, which caters for the health foods required by the devotees of the Manor, the home of the Krishna Consciousness religious sect. The village has now become the home of commuters, who leave the village daily to work in London or Watford. The local farm is now a private house, as are the Anglican Chapel and the village school. The little Methodist Chapel has also become a private house in 1985.

The only development in the parish since the Second World War was the building of a council estate and some private homes to the west of Radlett, encroaching into the eastern boundary of Aldenham parish. Further development has been strictly limited as the Green Belt and Conservation Areas restricted any movement out of the villages. Only some infilling is allowed and only when such building fits in with the environment of the area.

Anstey

In the old days, when I was young, the well was the very centre of village life; the women came to get water and gossip. The boys cut the wood under the well top and wrote verses and names; it was a

great thing to watch someone turning the big wheel to get water. We would watch them take their water, then nip up quick with our buckets and take what they had left, saving us a job of drawing more water up.

The men had a choice of five pubs; now only the Chequers is left. The Bell had a little old lady about four feet nothing. She used to wear long black skirts with a very white apron. She cooked her food over the bar fire and would leave off her rolling to serve the beer.

What fun we children had watching the hurdle maker at work; we went home with bundles of chips from the stakes. These were used to light the fire under the copper for hot water.

The butchers' shop was in the Chequers yard. The poor people used to go up with their trucks (a big wooden box on pram wheels) to get the offal and pigs' bellies. We paid two pence for a whole cart full. The general stores sold everything from a boot button to a yard of calico, baked bread in the brick oven at the back of the shop. We often got broken biscuits, and the sugar dust at the bottom of the jar. The shop stayed open till after eight o'clock.

There was a shoe maker and repairer at Snow End; we children watched him steep the leather in water; he used two needles to sew the sole on a shoe, then nails and very smelly black wax to go round the sole and heel. The shoes and boots were like new again.

In the 1930s we had a cycle shop at Pain's End, and could hire a bicycle for sixpence a day. We also had a post office and dairy then.

The village blacksmith was the great attraction. How we loved to blow the bellows to make the fire red and watch the horse shoes being made and the horses shod. It was a full time job as there were many farm horses then.

Anstey Fair which used to come every St. Swithun's time was the great excitement in our young lives. The stalls were erected along Cheap Side. Two pence was all we had to spend, but it was a lot of money to us children. The Fair stopped coming at the end of the 1920s, but now it has been revived and takes place in the Old Rectory Garden.

Northey wood and Scales are lovely woods; the deer roam in Scales, and there are still primroses, bluebells and cowslips in the spring and blackberries in the autumn. We children used to gather them all day in holidays and also help with the harvest and pea picking.

14

The gypsies lived down Bell Lane. I remember a little boy in 1922 coming to the door and singing his Christmas Carol:

'The Cock flew up the plum tree
The hen came whistling by,
I wish you a merry Christmas
with a fat pig in the sty.
The roads are very dirty
My shoes very thin
But I have a little pocket
To put some half pennies in.'

Ardeley

CAUTION – DRIVE SLOWLY – DUCKS CROSSING ROAD. This warning sign was my initial introduction to the delightful village of Ardeley twenty-eight years ago. The road in question lay between a pond close to the 13th century Church of St. Lawrence and the Church Hall, a thatched building matching several fairly large thatched houses which form a horseshoe circle bordering the Village Green. The houses were built as late as the 1920s and are unquestionably in character with the village. Indeed they are quite a feature and surely an inspiration of the architect: a fine example as to what can be achieved in any day and age if sufficient care and thought is given.

Visitors to Ardeley with its 13th-century church, its 17th-century Vicarage, its venerable pub and its village pond might well be forgiven if they took the village green, ringed with attractive white-walled, thatched cottages and village hall and centring on a substantial tiled well-head, to be of an earlier century than our own. In fact, houses, hall and well-head are all not much more than 65 years old.

Before the creation of the Green a mansion called Ardeley Place had stood on or near the site. This house, already in decay, had been demolished in the mid-nineteenth century.

The conception of the Green was due to a formidable partnership between two men, Mr. John Howard Carter of Ardeley Bury and the Reverend Dr. H. V. S. Eck, then Vicar of the Parish of Ardeley.

John Howard Carter had come to Ardeley when the family purchased the Bury and a considerable amount of land in the village in 1914. The previous owners had been the Scott family, one of whose daughters, Annie Josephine, had married the then Vicar, Mark Ruddock.

The land that was to become the Green formed part of the holdings of the Carters and building began in 1917. The two men had this vision of the village which they were determined should appear.

It may seem to have been a strange time to begin building. The 1914–18 War was at its bloodiest height. It took its toll of the young men of the village whose names stand commemorated on the Memorial opposite the Green. Yet in the midst of this carnage Mr. Carter and Dr. Eck had the vision to see that there would come an end to the fighting and that people would want to return to the peace of the English countryside to live in pleasant surroundings. It is perhaps an indication of this foresight that one of the houses bears the painted inscription *Auspicium melioris aevis* (A sign of better times). The first of the houses, All Hallows was completed in 1917 and its first occupants were the Sisters of the Community of St. Andrew to whom Mr. Carter lent it to be used as a rest house. The Sisters were anxious to be a useful part of the village and they remained helping here till they left in 1942. In all, the building of the houses took until 1920.

As a centre piece for the Green, Mr. Carter erected the well house, a sturdy hexagonal structure of brick and solid timbers topped by a tiled roof. The well was not merely decorative. It was to supply water to the residents of the Green for some years until the coming of piped water to the village. Although the well has not been used for a long time the machinery for raising water is still in place.

The other building standing on the Green is the Village Hall completed in 1919. This was very much the brain-child of Dr. Eck. As early as 1917 he had been writing in the Parish Magazine of the need for a meeting place for the people of the Parish. He had the charity to say that it should be for the use of all the villagers without distinction of religion. The land on which it was to be built was given by Mr. Carter while Dr. Eck assisted in raising the funds for the purchase and the actual building, although the people of the village contributed in many ways. Local farmers provided their horses and wagons to cart the materials from the nearest railway station whilst others found themselves digging the foundations. Dr. Eck had the knack of firing others with his own vigorous enthusiasm.

Later, the land and building were conveyed by Mr. Carter to the St. Albans Diocesan Board of Finance who acted as Trustees.

16

Work on the Hall was completed in 1919 and, in the November of the year after the cessation of hostilities, the Hall was officially opened by the then Lord Robert Cecil. A photograph of the occasion still hangs in the Hall and among the spectators shown are several present residents of the village.

There are no shops in Ardeley, but a warm community spirit ensures that those without transport are taken care of by willing car owners. Also a bus service is in operation twice a week.

Needless to say, there is a pub, The Jolly Waggoner, sporting a huge wheel in front of its attractive black and white facade. Small tables abound when the weather permits to welcome customers who drive over from neighbouring towns for country ale, atmosphere and bar snacks.

High on the outskirts of Ardeley stands Hertfordshire's only surviving post windmill. Its main support is reputed to be the largest single oak post in the county. Its 'sweeps' (sails) have been removed, but the main structure was immaculately restored in 1968 thus providing an unusual landmark for miles. Some of the elderly people remember its working days. One old farmer would laugh reflecting how, in his young days, he had to put sacks over his horses heads before they would pass the swirling sails!

The ducks and the caution sign have long since vanished, but the traditions of this enchanting little village remain. As we all know, nothing in this world is perfect, so of course those who live in the village have, like anywhere else, their own personal problems to face and there are occasional clashes of personalities. But to sum up, a shining friendliness abounds and as time has passed bringing births, deaths, departures of old friends, arrivals of newcomers, we have watched the pride with which Ardeley's homes and gardens are kept, the modernization a few years ago of the ever popular school, the many events given in the Church Hall, and last, but certainly not least, our ever growing, enthusiastic and very much alive W.I.

Arkley 🦡

Compared with many Hertfordshire villages, Arkley is quite young, but the name 'Arkleysland' is mentioned in historical records of 1332. It was described as land on the West of Barnet Common where a few peasants had made a clearing for dwellings, cultivated strips of field and established a small community. At this time, the land belonged to St. Albans Abbey, and the Abbot was Lord of the Manor. He was reputed to have held his Manor Court at the west end of the Common near where two of our famous landmarks now stand. The Gate public house, originally The Bell, and the Arkley Windmill.

As Manor Courts were usually held at an Inn and the sign of a bell indicated the site of an Abbot's Court, it is very likely that the present Inn is in the same place. County records show that a certain John Gillet was granted a licence in the year 1752 to 'serve refreshment at the Bell at the Gate'. The 'gate' was across the western entrance to the Common to 'keep in beasts that had been led there to graze', not a tollgate.

It is difficult to imagine 100 years ago our busy Barnet Road was a small path across a Common where children would run into their houses if a stranger walked through the gate on the way to Barnet, so few people ever passed by.

Bell Cottage, across the road from The Gate, demolished in 1972, was described in 1860 as 'a wretched hovel to which the widow who had kept The Bell for many years was sent by the brewery to live in her old age'. The Gate and Bell Cottage had been a local landmark for years especially as their proximity caused the Barnet Road to narrow considerably and made it difficult for two vehicles to pass. Close by in the gardens of Blue Hills stands the Arkley Windmill 22 metres high, offering a fine view from its wooden gallery of Harrow-on-the-Hill, Aylesbury and far into London. The original Windmill was built in 1806 when corn prices were high owing to the Napoleonic Wars. Not only local farmers but the people of Arkley and nearby Barnet brought their corn to be ground. Many people grew their own corn as they could not afford to buy flour.

Some of the older residents of Arkley still remember going to the mill to buy flour. It ceased to be a working mill in 1917 and fell into disrepair. In 1929 it was repaired with only two sails. More repairs were effected but one sail blew off in a gale on Christmas Day 1958 and the other on Derby Day a year later. Once more the mill was renovated and fitted with four sails, but a sail snapped in a gale in 1974. Its present owners with some help from Barnet Council repaired the windmill in 1985. It is a listed building but the Preservation Order, unfortunately, carries no protection from the elements!

The Arkley Windmill is considered to be the finest of only five working windmills in the Home Counties. A very old Barnet saying 'He's never been out of sight of the windmill', implies a very limited outlook.

Our other listed building at the eastern end of the village in Galley Lane is a barn dating from 1625. It forms part of the buildings of Elm Farm, where during recent renovations a Jocobean fireplace and a bread oven were uncovered. The barn is particularly interesting for it was built of brick, very rare at this time as neither river nor canal passed through Arkley to bring bricks into the area. This suggests that the brickfields were already established. There were three brickfields within a mile of Arkley. This resulted in an increase in the population of Arkley, and the first village community was formed. The agriculture and brickwork were seasonal and when the weather was bad pay was suspended. A few rich gentlemen lived in the area. One in particular, Enosh Durant of High Cannons near Shenley became the benefactor of Arkley Village. He built the church of local brick, dedicated to St. Peter on 1st November 1840. He added a school and schoolmistress's house, these are now the church hall and vicarage. He provided the girls with lilac print pinafores and the boys with Holland smocks. These had to be taken home on Friday, washed and starched ready for school on Monday. All the Durant household attended morning service each Sunday. They took an interest in the whole community. At Christmas red flannel was distributed to the old ladies whilst the old men received dark coats. The local farmers sent a joint of beef to each family and there were oranges for the children.

The Village Hall is a recent addition to our community life, opened in 1969. It was built with subscriptions started before the last war by the Arkley Girls' Club and added to from fund raising efforts by the various village organisations, well-wishers and Barnet Council. It is situated in Brickfield Lane across from The Gate and beside the Windmill. This is where most of the social activities of the village take place.

Ashwell

> 'Some Ashen trees and water bubbling, springing
> Just where the chalky hillside meets the plain,
> And gathered all about them clustering clinging
> The village homesteads have for ages lain.'

Skirting the village to the south is Icknield Way, an ancient thoroughfare of prehistoric times which may have accounted for the early importance of the settlement. Also passing to the south of Ashwell is another old way, locally called the Ruddery and known to be a Roman road, Ashwell Street.

It may come as some surprise to follow any of the six roads which today will bring you into the village of Ashwell to see the tower of the Church of St. Mary the Virgin rising so high from such a small village. Tucked away in the north east corner of fertile Hertfordshire countryside, Ashwell had a regular market in the Middle Ages and, at the time of the Norman invasion, was sixth town in the county. For close on a thousand years, Ashwell has had an intimate connection with Westminster Abbey. The foundations and present church date from the 14th century. To the chancel a precise date can be given. In 1368 a document in the Muniment Room at Westminster Abbey refers to the Abbey paying £118.7s.8d. as their share of the cost.

The walls of the church tower were about 12ft. high when the Black Death raging over Europe reached Ashwell, and all work on it stopped for several years. On the north wall is scratched some Latin graffiti which, translated, reads: '1350 – miserable wild distracted the dregs of the people alone survive to witness and tell the tale and in the end with a tempest Maurus this year thunders mightily in all the world 1361'. This no doubt refers to the storm on St. Maur's day 15th January 1361 which may have cleared the air of the last lingering infection of the Death.

A medieval architect records his disapproval on the first pillar near the south door which, translated, reads 'the corners are not pointed correctly – I spit at them'.

In more recent times when Ashwell Feast was celebrated, so much cleaning and polishing was done that visitors coming down the hill into Ashwell, it was said, met all the spiders leaving the village.

There can be few villages in England, let alone Hertfordshire, which can boast a post lady quite like Mrs Flo Worboys. Until her retirement at the age of 87 due to a knee injury which made cycling no longer possible, she was a familar sight delivering the post. In recognition of her service to the community, she was awarded the British Empire Medal after 61 years and a quarter of a million miles of pedalling round the lanes of Ashwell.

Another claim to fame for the village was its watercress which grew at Ashwell Springs which used to be taken to London regularly and there sold to the sound of one of the old London Street cries 'Ashwell Hed Watercrease'.

In 1928, Mr John Sale of Farrows Farm found a novel way of expressing his thanks and appreciation for what the *Daily Mail* did for farmers. He grew a crop of mustard in the shape of the words 'Thank you Daily Mail'. Each letter was 47 yards long and 6 yards wide and the general effect printed on a square of 4 or 5 acres was easily seen from the road. He enlisted the help of two others and two and a half days were given to the work of laying out the letters with string and sowing the seed.

Firing the Anvil was a very old Ashwell custom. At midnight on 5th November after fireworks had been let off, in Primes Yard was placed an anvil and some gun powder put on it. Three or four times this was done and set fire to, the loud bangs being heard all over the village.

Beating the Bounds or the Perambulation on Ascension Day was also a very old custom when the people went round the village beating the bounds. At certain points, a child would be bumped up and down on a stone. A note of this in 1635 reads 'when money was payed for bred kake and beer at the peramble of the village'.

Aston

Aston is one of the smaller small villages in Hertfordshire: some 280 houses, with an electoral roll around 660; now dwarfed and somewhat menaced by neighbouring Stevenage New Town whose tentacles extend to within yards of the common boundary.

Shown on early maps as Estone or Easton (presumably in contrast to Weston, a much larger village to the north and west) its history can be traced back to the late 11th century when the Bury (i.e. Manor) of Aston was given to Bishop Odo of Bayeux, brother of the Conqueror. He fell from grace in 1088 and the land and title reverted to the crown for the next 50 years until the widow of Henry I gifted the manor to the Benedictine Abbey at Reading, exhorting them to pray for the King's soul, his progenitors and successors in perpetuity. The monks founded a 'daughter house' in Aston and remnants of this monastery can still be discerned in the cellars and foundations of the present building, Astonbury, on the site, together with a well under the hall floor, and some flintwork in the lower part of the outside walls.

At the Dissolution of the Monasteries in 1536 the monks were expelled and four years later the Manor of Aston – including the monastery buildings – was granted to Sir Philip Boteler of Watton Woodhall, who had been one of the knights of the Body to King Henry VIII. He built the main part of the present house, and his grandson John added the two great staircases on the south wall. The majority of the windows are on the north wall which makes for a rather sunless interior, but the reason for this is interesting – it was a widely held belief at that time that the plague blew in from the south and therefore it was safer to keep a solid wall of protection.

In 1564 Sir John Boteler sold a piece of his land to one Thomas Waterman and some of the oldest cottages in Aston date from this period. Solomon's Pightle – a row of four cottages (now three) has recently been re-roofed, but to all outward appearance has not changed in 400 years! The cottages opposite in Benington Road are currently being restored, but the relics of their past, such as the cruck frame, the old baker's oven and some wall-paintings discovered during the restoration are being carefully preserved.

There appears to have been little building between Elizabethan and Victorian times, but fortunately both at Aston and Aston End, a number of listed buildings have been carefully restored – including a genuine Elizabethan cottage which still retains its thatched roof. Aston House itself was demolished over 20 years ago, having been sadly neglected but it had its claim to fame as one of the top secret military establishments during World War II.

There was a certain amount of building between the wars – mostly in the public sector – but by far the greatest expansion has been over the last 25 years with one quite large and five smaller housing developments on the fringes of the village. Strenuous efforts are being made to keep the field in the centre of the village intact and preserved for posterity.

Shopping facilities are adequate, if exiguous: a sub-post office which also caters for almost 'all the human frame requires' and an elegant antique shop which no self-respecting village should be without. While at Aston End there are no less than two chicken and egg farms, and an obliging family butcher. For fresh fish one must go farther afield. Three pubs are well patronised (there were actually six in an earlier day).

The population is an interesting cross section of old villagers – some names like Pallett, Wright and Chalkley go back several hundred years – and newcomers, many of whom play a considerable part in the 22 clubs and societies listed in the village directory. There is something for everyone, from a pre-school playgroup to the Over-60s Club, badminton and bowls, tennis and theatricals, and a well-known team of bell-ringers. Also included of course is Aston W.I. which celebrated its 65th anniversay in 1985, and is very much a moving force in the village with members taking part in, and sometimes instigating services such as the Mother and Baby clinic, the prescription rota and care of the War Memorial.

Ayot St. Lawrence 🦡

The first record of Ayot St. Lawrence is in the reign of King Edward the Confessor, when, according to Chauncy, it was part of the possessions of Earl Harold – afterwards King Harold. When Harold was defeated at the Battle of Hastings, the land and manor came into the possession of William the Conqueror, and after changing hands many times, reverted to the crown in 1538. In King Henry VIII's reign it was occupied by Sir Richard Parr, whose daughter Catherine was reputedly courted there by the King.

Passing through various baronial hands, Sir Lionel Lyde, a wealthy tobacco merchant from Bristol, acquired the lordship of the manor in the 1770s. A colourful figure, he abandoned the original tudor manor and built himself a typical early Georgian redbrick mansion nearby in the park. Not content with this, he began to demolish the old village church, which dated from the 12th century, because it obstructed the view from his new mansion. Not surprisingly the Bishop of Lincoln, in whose diocese the parish then was, objected to this and further demolition was prevented, giving the village a picturesque, ivy-covered ruin, a favourite subject for artists and photographers.

Sir Lionel was also obliged to erect a new parish church, which the famous architect Nicholas Revett built in flamboyant, neo-classical style. It is said that the portico of this new palladian church was a copy of the Temple of Apollo at Delos. Sir Lionel certainly did not want anyone to spoil his view of this famous portico, and therefore the villagers had to approach the church from behind, and enter by a side door. Attached to the portico are colonnades ending in open pavilions, and containing the tombs of Sir Lionel and his wife – one at each end. This unusual arrangement was the result of a life of marital strife – Sir Lionel having vowed that the church which had united them in life should make amends by separating them in death. In more recent times Sir Lionel's mansion – Ayot House – became the refuge of ex-King Michael of Roumania during the Second World War, and afterwards a silk farm, where the silk for the Prince of Wales' investiture robes and for the royal Christening gowns was produced.

The New Rectory cannot claim to be a famous building architecturally, but was for almost 50 years the home of the most famous resident of Ayot St. Lawrence, George Bernard Shaw. He came to Ayot because he loved its peace and stillness – the roads were not metalled until 1936 – and because he was impressed by the longevity of so many of its inhabitants. A tombstone in its churchyard reads 'Mary Anne South, born 1825, died 1895. Her time was short.' And this came true for G.B.S. – who lived until the age of 94 and died in Ayot in November 1950 after falling from a ladder while pruning trees. Here in Ayot he lived happily with his wife Charlotte; here he wrote his later works like *Pygmalion, Heartbreak House, Back to Methuselah, Saint Joan* and many others; and here he received many famous visitors from all over the world. The Webbs and other Fabians came, writers and actors came. And Lawrence of Arabia came too – a great friend of Charlotte and G.B.S.

George Bernard Shaw left his house to the National Trust and the rooms in which he lived and worked are now preserved for the Nation, bringing many visitors to Ayot St. Lawrence. Every year in July the Shaw Society commemorates his birthday with a weekend of short plays performed on the lawn of his house – 'Shaw's Corner' – as a fitting memorial to this great dramatist. Another annual tribute to the Arts is the Ayot St. Lawrence Midsummer Festival, consisting of an art exhibition and concerts in the palladian church – a graceful setting for local talent in this beautiful part of Hertfordshire.

Ayot St. Peter ✤

Totally overshadowed by its more famous neighbour Ayot St. Lawrence, Ayot St. Peter is granted little more than two lines in learned reference books. Yet coming up the B197 and crossing the busy A1(M) over a bridge, suddenly a peaceful village green opens up, crossed by narrow lanes flanked by old oak and chestnut trees – Ayot Green. The old cottages around the Green used to belong to farm labourers working on the nearby estates. Now they have been converted lovingly into charming residences and the strict planning laws of this conservation area have ensured tasteful modernisations.

Crossing the Green the fine red-brick spire of Ayot St. Peter comes into view, a church built in the Early Decorated Style with a tiled roof crested in terra-cotta. A church built in 1874/75 and the fourth church of Ayot St. Peter. Can many English villages boast of having had four churches? Little is known of the first medieval church except that by the middle of the 18th century it had become so costly to repair it, that it was thought more economic to replace it. In 1751 the Rector of the Parish, the Rev. Dr. Freman got permission to rebuild the church in a curious octagonal shape with a separate belfry forming the entrance to the churchyard. But fashions changed and by 1850 the 'pagan' architecture of the previous century condemned this church as having 'more the aspect of a lock-up'. The then incumbent of the parish, the Rev. Edwin Prodgers and his son – both men of private means from a living in Ireland – decided to build a new church at a cost of nearly £2000 – mostly from their own pockets. Yet this church had an even shorter life than the previous one, for on 10th July 1874 its roof was struck by lightning and set ablaze, and by next morning only a burned-out shell remained. The rector had managed to save the church plate and registers but little else. However, this tragedy was a blessing in disguise. Lord Cowper, a local landowner, gave some land much closer to the village and with the help of an insurance claim on the burned building and with generous subscriptions from local dignitaries a new church was designed by the famous architect John Pollard Seddon and put into service in October 1875. Eventually the old site and churchyard was abandoned and is now a charming jumble of plant and wildlife, with rabbits jumping over the fallen gravestones and skylarks nesting amongst the ivy and wild flowers.

At the end of the last century the steam railway threatened to bring Ayot St. Peter into the modern world, for in 1860 a railway was opened between Hatfield, Luton and Dunstable. Nearby Welwyn Garden City did then not exist, so Ayot Station became an important stop on the new line. This branch line was a large undertaking and the stretch between Luton and Hatfield took two years to complete, giving employment to local labour. Most hard-working of those must have been the navvies, with two navvies expected to shovel 20 tons of rock and earth per day for a weekly wage of 15 shillings (75p). Once completed, the railway brought great advantages to local industries and at peak times Vauxhall Motors of Luton sent two 40-wagon train loads of cars per day on the new line. Passenger traffic was important too, with special trains to Harpenden for the annual horse races there, and seaside excursion trains to Skegness, Yarmouth and Clacton – the third class return fare from Ayot to Clacton was 8 shillings (40p). However, in July 1948 Ayot Station was destroyed by fire and never rebuilt and closed to passenger traffic in the next year. Under Dr. Beeching's economies the whole branch line closed in 1965 and after all the rails were finally removed the County Council acquired the land. It is now the Ayot Greenway – a delightful walk and bridle way of about 2½ miles from Ayot to Wheathampstead, giving extensive views of the rolling countryside and the Lee valley, and harbouring a richness of wildlife.

Though mentioned in the Domesday Book as part of the land owned by the Norman Baron Robert Gernon; though decimated by smallpox in 1770; though having had three churches destroyed, history has left Ayot St. Peter largely untouched. The railway came and went; the population fell when agriculture declined, the little village school closed and more recently the village shop too. In 1973 the building of the A1(M) cut off a part of the village including the village hall – but here again Ayot was fortunate since the motorway is in a deep cutting hidden from view. What has grown out of the past is a very peaceful and lovely village and perhaps because most inhabitants work in the towns, they are anxious to preserve and enhance this particularly beautiful part of the Hertfordshire countryside.

26

Barkway 🐚

The village of Barkway lies in the eastern extension of the chalky Chiltern Hills. In prehistoric times it was the site of a major crossroads – the east–west trading route taking advantage of the dry highlands of the scarp and the north–south track linking London with Cambridge and, eventually, Kings Lynn.

There is much evidence of man's early existence close to the crossroads and slightly to the east, on the banks of the river Quin, where deposits of flint flakes and half-finished tools suggest a sophisticated settlement and trading station. To the west of the London–Cambridge road lies Periwinkle Hill. This ancient and now almost lost mound was probably the base of a strong point and lookout tower giving a fine view across the plains of Cambridgeshire as far as the settlement of Ely.

The conquest of Britain by the Romans left its mark on the surrounding landscape; Barkway, however, was left untouched save only for one small cache of Roman silver found at the edge of nearby Rookey Wood, during the 18th century.

The Norman invasion brought a new culture and a new light to England. Probably the Chiltern edge was used by William as a springboard for his troops as they prepared to suppress the uprising of Hereward and his compatriots in the Fenlands of Cambridgeshire and Lincolnshire. William, a true bureaucrat and undisputed head of the Norman civil service, decreed that he should know the full extent of the wealth of the land and have an exact record of Crown property. In 1086, exactly nine hundred years ago, he instituted the Domesday Survey. This crushing census was carried out with meticulous attention to detail and not a village or homestead was missed. Barkway was examined in detail and for the first time its name appeared on an official document. Apart from the farming commitments, the village partly supported a 'holy man' – probably one of the few villagers capable of reading and writing and so elevated to a position of authority. He was able to communicate with the ecclesiastical courts and so was given the title of 'Priest'. His Church would have been no more than a small wooden structure – just sufficient to have housed him, a few members of his congregation and his farm animals – perhaps a goat and a few chickens. The community only partially supported him and he was expected to 'do his bit'.

Barkway flourished – it was granted a market and so became an important trading point and a place for social gathering. Despite being ravaged by major fires in the 15th and 18th centuries, it became one of the major stopping points on the coaching route from London to the north east. The inhabitants became wealthy and complacent and were unconcerned about the gradual decline of the coach trade in the mid 1800s. A railway was proposed with a station between Barkway and Reed – the engineer was Robert Stephenson. However it failed to materialise and Barkway became a backwater.

By the turn of the 20th century, Barkway was like so many other Hertfordshire villages – away from the main roads and therefore away from the attention of the County authorities. Slipping further and further into a decline, the population slumped as the people sought their fortunes in Royston and, sometimes, London.

The Second World War brought a resurgence of importance with the building of the airfield at nearby Nuthampstead but when peace came, the decline returned with renewed vigour. Today Barkway's fifteen shops have been reduced to a very small single outlet – the twenty or so pubs and beerhouses reduced to two. The school roll barely reaches 50 – it was over a hundred in the 1800s. What now is the future of Barkway? Are we, also, complacent about its future? Barkway is a village with a past – it needs a clear perspective to survive.

Barley

Barley is a small village on the chalk slopes at the end of the Chilterns and Royston people refer to us as 'The Little Men' from the hills. This could well be true as according to Mr. Jack Wilkerson, Barley was flourishing before Julius Caesar came to Britain; evidence was found in 1959 of an Iron Age farm site.

I wonder what these people would think of Barley today? Walking into the one village shop they would be astonished at the display of goods; everything from frozen food to coal plus the Post Office and friendly assistants.

People tend to associate Barley with the *Fox and Hounds* sign which spans the road from pub to forge. The forge is now used to repair and renovate vintage cars. One often sees an old crock arriving which in time emerges restored to its former glory. This, in some way, seems to continue the work of the Old Forge which until only a few years ago was a very busy blacksmiths.

Village activities range from Cubs to Over-sixties, also a very active local riding school, so all ages are catered for. The Barley Players produce two excellent shows a year – Christmas pantomime and a summer show. They are extremely talented and very well supported by the whole village. The summer show is held in the Barn at Lower Yard and the music and laughter can be heard throughout the village – a lovely happy sound on a summer's evening. The pantomime is performed in the Town House which is our local Hall. The Town House has two floors, the main upper floor and an undercroft. Built in the 1600s it has been used as a courthouse, workhouse, almshouse and the first school. The old hand-worked fire engine was kept in the undercroft and the original *Fire Engine* sign still hangs there. The undercroft of our Town House had, over the years, fallen into decay but has now been renovated and the transformation from a dark damp room to the light pleasant beamed hall is due mainly to hardworking volunteers and the generosity of the village. The Town House is the centre for most village activities. Meetings are held there, Parish Council, British Legion, W.I., visits from our local M.P. etc., also exhibitions and a monthly country market. Held mainly upstairs, are dances, discos, Harvest Suppers and of course wedding receptions as the church is immediately across the road.

Folks who return to Barley after a long absence are delighted it has retained its character and if anything is more attractive. The name itself conjures up a very pretty village.

Bayford 🦢

Bayford, owned by Edward the Confessor, remained a royal possession for centuries after the Norman Conquest – at one time it belonged to Edward III's son, John of Gaunt, after whom an ancient oak in the Manor House grounds is named. In 1544, Henry VIII granted it to the Knighton family, who were squires for nearly one hundred years. The next significant event was the sale of the Manor in 1757 by the family of Caesar (who had a relative named Julius!) to Sir William Baker M.P., a wealthy merchant and Alderman of the City of London, who had the new mansion of Bayfordbury built in the north of the parish and surrounded by a fine ornamental park. For nearly two hundred years, he and his descendants not only improved the estate but were benefactors in the parish.

The Bakers were all enthusiastic planters of trees, providing Bayford with a heritage it still largely preserves; the huge cedars of Lebanon surround the house to this day as do most of the belts of woodland encircling the park, though some, such as Weepings Wood, have been largely felled in recent years and many hedgerows removed in pursuit of modern methods of farming, thereby changing the face of parts of the parish, as did the disappearance of the many fine elms due to Dutch Elm Disease. One very ancient woodland remains in the park, Hook's Grove, named after Ralph Hoke, a friend of John of Gaunt's, containing some fine conifers, including redwoods, planted by the family. The crowning glory, though, must be the famous Bayfordbury Pinetum, an outstanding collection of exotic pines, begun in 1838 by William Robert Baker in consultation with John Claudius Loudun, then the foremost authority on landscape gardening.

The Bakers replaced the old parish Church, which was in a poor state of repair, first in 1804, and then in 1871 with a permanent and beautifully built and appointed structure on a slightly different site (leaving some graves, including the Baker vault, outside in the churchyard). It is a fine example of Victorian church design by Henry Woodyer, a pupil of the well-known William Butterfield.

In 1913, Henry Clinton Baker presented Bayford with its Memorial Hall (to the memory of his father), still the parish hall today and the centre of many activities, including the monthly meetings of the W.I.

Bedmond ✍

Life in Bedmond could date back as far as the early Stone Age as findings of one or two Palaeolithic implements were recorded in the last century. Certainly some sort of settlement must have existed as early as 1100 because history records that Nicholas Breakspear, the only English Pope, was born in Bedmond about that time. He became Pope Adrian 1V from 1154–1159. In the grounds of Breakspeare Farm, his reputed birthplace, was a spring, marked on early maps as a Holy Well. It was said that the water contained healing properties for the eyes and it became a place of pilgrimage. In time, the original building was replaced by another Breakspeare farm but all that remains today is a plaque dedicated to Nicholas Breakspeare situated near the site of the farm.

In the mid 19th century, Bedmond was a hamlet of about one hundred cottages. The roads were gravel tracks and there was no electricity, running water or sanitation. It qualified for the name 'village' in 1880 when its own Church of England was built: the Church of the Ascension. There was a Baptist Chapel prior to this, but villagers who wished to worship in a Church of England had to walk the mile to St. Lawrence in Abbots Langley. The building of the iron church in Bedmond, unique because it is the only one of its kind with a spire, was financed by Mr. William Solly, who was the Squire of Abbots Langley, but who lived in Serge Hill House in Bedmond. It was built 'so that the spiritual lives of those residing in Bedmond shall go forth with increased vigour'. Services are still held twice a month and on special festivals. Mr. and Mrs. Solly performed many good works for the village.

The Serge Hill Estate was vast and comprised seven farms. Many men of the village worked on the Estate in one capacity or another until it was sold in the early part of this century. Mr. Solly died in 1886 after founding the Solly Trust which was the investment of a large sum of money, the profit of which was to be divided among the five most needy and worthy villagers twice a year. This charity still functions today in the capable hands of its Trustees.

There are two very old Public Houses still flourishing in the village. The Bell, formerly known as The Blue Bell, was probably established about 1618 and The White Hart may have been an ale house since 1733. There were others too, the most notorious of which was The Travellers' Rest, reputed to be a regular stopping place for Dick Turpin. Apparently there was a huge fireplace with steps leading up the chimney to the roof where Turpin would hide. The cellars had been converted into stables, but the space was so limited that there was no room for the horses to turn and they had to be led out backwards!

The Travellers' Rest stood in Porridge Pot Hill. One explanation for that delightful name is that porridge seems to have been the staple refreshment for travellers. The other is based on the whimsical legend that a witch lived in the dip at the bottom of the hill and the strange smoke-like mist which gathered in the dip on autumn mornings (and still does!) was the steam rising from her porridge!

That same witch, according to legend, was also responsible for the stoniness of the soil in Bedmond as apparently, after once getting very angry, she cursed the ground and it became stony. Porridge Pot Hill was changed by the Council to Church Hill about twenty years ago, saddening many residents as the link with the past was severed.

In one of the cottage gardens near The Travellers' Rest stood a huge yew cross. It seems that the owner of the cottage who was a master carpenter, was also keen on topiary. He planted three yew trees hoping to train them to represent the feathers of the Prince of Wales. Unfortunately one tree died, so he wired the others together in the shape of a cross and it eventually stood about 20 feet high with a circumference of nearly 35 feet. Sadly this landmark disappeared, along with The Travellers' Rest and the cottages with the march of 'progress'.

Another Bedmond feature was a large pond where farmers would fill their water carts and where sheep were washed prior to being driven along the road to market in Watford or St. Albans. Rumour says that gravel was dug from that area by French soldiers to help in the building of St. Albans Abbey and that the huge dip left behind was gradually filled up by springs to form a natural pond. The pond has now gone and the area is planted with trees.

At the edge of the village near Abbots Langley stood the Ovaltine Dairy Farm; a beautiful black and white thatched building, part of which was a copy of the model dairy farm which Marie Antoinette owned in Versailles. Recently, however, the farm was sold and the M25 now pushes through what was the rich grazing land for the farm's Jersey cows. The building has been converted to private dwellings and is appropriately named Antoinette Court.

Bedmond is a thriving village and we are confident that it will remain so whatever changes are destined for the future.

Bengeo 🪶

Old maps show original Bengeo as a small area around the Church of St. Leonards, Revels farm, a Manor house and two cottages. These still stand today. The Manor house became the rectory. One of the cottages, still thatched, has a flint wall as

The Pest House, Bengeo.

does the church, and it is believed was a hunting lodge, whilst the other was a hostelry. Bengeo Hall, or Rectory, its origins over 500 years old, is a timber-framed building with later additions. The fir-covered hillside, atop which the church was built, and now known as the Warren, looks down on the meads below where archery was practised during the 16th century. There was also a small vineyard, from which the cottages take their name.

On the western slope lies the 'Pest House', now a private home, but once an isolation hospital for small-pox, used in the 18th century by Thomas Dimsdale, who lived adjacent and who experimented with inoculation. This worthy gentleman was to become Baron Dimsdale as a result of inoculating Queen Catherine, Empress of Russia, and her family. It was his descendants who speculatively developed land to the west; this, no doubt, speeded by the coming of the railway in 1859.

Bengeo, once truly rural, still maintains a village atmosphere, surrounded as it is by beautiful countryside and some of its inhabitants are still dependent upon the soil, as is recorded in poems by Corporal Lobb of the Bengeo Home Guard, written during the Second World War.

'We possess countless privates called Vigus
And it is not that they don't li'gus,
They are absent from drill
And we know that they will
Milk their cows first, then fight like old tigers'.

Borehamwood 🦢

The railway became the 'lifeline' which turned Borehamwood from a village to a town and today it is still a very popular means of transport, carrying residents to the centre of London in about 20 minutes. There has been a great deal of controversy regarding the station's name. Originally, it was called 'Elstree' after the next village which was historically well known having been built along Watling Street, the old Roman road from London to St. Albans, whereas Borehamwood village was of practically no significance. As the village grew in importance many residents felt the station should be called Borehamwood and after a great deal of discussion the station was renamed Elstree and Borehamwood; but now the name 'Elstree' has reappeared.

Shenley Road is now the main thoroughfare of the town, with to the north and south, two London County Council (later Greater London Council) estates, local Council and private houses, mostly built since the 1939/45 war.

In Shenley Road stands All Saints (C. of E.) Church built in 1910. Borehamwood caters for people of every denomination or belief. Adjacent to the church is the community hall which is a popular place for jumble sales and bazaars. It is, at present, in a poor state of repair, but we understand plans are in hand for a redevelopment of the whole site. This hall was purchased by the employees of Wellington and Ward who contributed a shilling a week to buy a 'brick'. When the necessary money had been raised the hall erected was identical to the one that Wellington and Ward had bought for their employees' social activities.

Opposite the hall, just off the main road, lies the B.B.C. Television Studios, where if one peeps around one can see the set of the current weekly series 'The Eastenders'. Previously the buildings were occupied by I.T.V., and before that the National Film Studios. The film industry came to Borehamwood early in 1914 as the air was right and the railway made it easily accessible. Neptune, Gates, M.G.M. and Associated British were some of the studios in the district. In the early days many of the local residents were employed as extras, and even today folk still enjoy watching shots being taken in the vicinity, or seeing on their television a well known part of the district. All studios were known as 'Elstree' not 'Borehamwood'.

The Women's Institute which started life in the quiet little village of Borehamwood now meets in the middle of a thriving prosperous town of 27,500 people.

Bourne End ✑

The Buckinghamshire Bourne End is graced by the rolling Thames; our Hertfordshire Bourne End is no less proud of its own 'river' – the diminutive Bourne Gutter. In former times, when this flash stream made one of its spasmodic appearances, it was thought to be a 'woe-water', or portent of war.

The many delightful Ends of this part of West Hertfordshire were celebrated in Victorian times by a local poet (J. Salter).

> 'There is Hottsmere End,
> And Revel End
> Bennetts End by the kiln,
> And Potten End,
> And Harper's End
> And Bourne End by the mill . . . .'

The Domesday mill, then called 'Whelpes-Bourne', has today been transformed into a motel, but the mill wheel and race can still be seen. The chalk stream that feeds the nearby Grand Union Canal still sparkles on its unhurried way, past pollarded willows and buttercup filled meadows, making this part of the valley of the river Bulbourne a pleasant 'overnight stop'.

The busy A41 divides the village into two distinct halves. Old fashioned hospitality can be enjoyed at the two neighbouring public houses, whilst the third is nowadays serving less alcoholic beverages in its 20th century guise as a 'Little Chef'.

The former watercress beds, for which the area was once renowned, are now a thriving Trout Farm, managed by the Sharp family. Three generations have lived in the cottage in 'Sharpes Lane' and played their part in the life of the community.

The peace of the area was somewhat disturbed in the late 18th and early 19th centuries when the canal and railway were constructed. The bridge over the canal, locally known as 'Battles Bridge' reminds us of those frenetic days when the navvies spent their spare time carousing or fighting – or adding to the list of casualties at the West Herts Infirmary!

The Roman Akeman Street passed through the parish, the canal and railway followed suit, utilising this gap in the Chiltern hills. During the coaching era, the inns along the Turnpike Road were much in demand. All these have come and gone without disturbing the inner peace and intrinsic beauty evident in our two adjacent valleys of the Bulbourne and Bourne Brook Gutter. Will the proposed By-pass to the A41 soon despoil the area William Cobbett described long ago as 'a pleasure ground' where 'the country children never looked better clad, cleaner or fatter than they look here'?

Bovingdon 🐝

Bovingdon is an attractive village situated on the edge of the Chilterns. Ancient British tumuli have been found in the area and there are also the remains of Roman villas at the Boxmoor end of the Parish.

There was at one time a thriving cottage industry of straw plaiting for the hat industry. The straw was brought from Luton to 'The Well' and people would collect it there and work at home. They sat on stools and had a tin underneath the stool with burning charcoal in it to keep them warm in winter as no fires were allowed in case the smoke discoloured the straw; for the same reason the plaiters had to see that their petticoats covered the stool and the charcoal tin. The plait would then be collected and taken to Luton for the hat trade.

During the last fifty years the population has grown from 500 to 5,000 so it is now a very large village.

The first church was built in 1235 but it did not become a separate parish until 1833. Up to that time Bovingdon and Flaunden were served by Hemel Hempstead Parish and the story is told of Bovingdon Sextons climbing the church tower on the fourth

Sunday of the month to watch for the Curate riding his horse through Stoney Lane. When he was sighted the bells were rung.

When Rev. A. Brooking was appointed Vicar in 1841 he found the church in a very bad state of repair and it was decided that it would be as cheap to pull it down and rebuild as to repair it. This work took 23 months and it was reopened in 1846. Part of the tower however is the original. The rebuilding cost £1,590.

The churchyard is one of the largest in Hertfordshire and contains some very fine avenues of yew trees, which, being poisonous, are supposed to have been planted to stop the vicar grazing his animals as well as to improve the appearance.

The prettiest part of the village is 'The Well' which was built in 1881 in memory of Granville Dudley Ryder who was Lord of the Manor and whose family lived in Westbrook Hay. Westbrook Hay was mentioned in histories of the time of King John but the present house was built about 1670. Its lodge in Hempstead Road was built in 1851 and is a flint and brick building containing several pieces of Hertfordshire puddingstone in its walls.

Near the Well is Bovingdon Docks. This is a spring forming a pond and is so called because in olden times villagers bragged that boats could dock in the centre of the village. This part of the village is liable to flooding after heavy rain. The last occasion being June 1982, but the worst flood was in 1946 when men from the local airfield came with dinghies to rescue people from nearby cottages.

The airfield was made during the Second World War and was used by American Airmen and later by the R.A.F. Some days four-engine bombers would leave for Germany at the rate of one every two minutes and seemed as though they would hit the chimneys of the houses in their flight path. One day a plane crash landed with a load of Italian cherries on board. Bovingdon children had a whale of a time!

Boxmoor ൠ

The name Boxmoor probably derived from the Box trees native to chalky down-land areas. Boxwood was used by the London block-makers or even in Cumberland to rub, when boiled, on a man's head to stop him going bald!

'Mor' signifies a marshy spot. These ancient water-meadows are still an important feature of the area. In 1574 they were given by

CHEMIST SHOP BOXMOOR 1900

Queen Elizabeth I to her court favourite, the Earl of Leicester, in return for favours we can only surmise!

'Castle Meade' and 'Bayley Meade' were later sold to three local inhabitants – John Rolfe, yeoman, Richard Pope, shoemaker, and William Gladman, yeoman, for the sum of £75. The money appears to have been raised by a secret public subscription. Thus came into being the Boxmoor Trust which, under an Act of Parliament dated 1809, continues to this day to administer and protect over 230 acres of common land in the vicinity.

There are twelve Trustees, publicly elected for life. Whilst the old-established rights of pasture are still subscribed for, the most important task of the Trust today is to keep this beautiful and unique heritage as an unspoilt 'green lung' for the urban communities that surround it.

The canal arrived on the scene in the late 18th century and cut its picturesque way through the valley, followed by the London to Birmingham Railway in 1837. Boxmoor Station was then the first stop from Euston and marquees were erected on 'Rowdown' Common, overlooking this new wonder of the age of steam. 'Gongoozlers' (a canal term) came to gawp at the iron monsters crossing the Turnpike Road on the famous skew bridge at Boxmoor.

Passengers on those early trains would have passed the spot where, in 1802, one Robert, or 'Robber' Snooks (christened James Snook) was hanged at the scene of his crime. He stopped the postboy and took the mailbags, but justice eventually caught up with him and he swung for his crime from the gallows tree. No one would pay for a coffin for his burial, so he was wrapped in straw and committed to the marshy ground. Two white-painted stones today mark the supposed place of his burial on the Moor near Bourne End. It is said that if you run round his grave three times calling his name, he will appear before you!

The railway, in effect, brought about the development of Boxmoor village. Before that, a cluster of old farmhouses, cottages, taverns and a shop in an area known as 'Crouchfield' were virtually all that existed here. The railway station took its original name from the common land that stretched beside it. Then an elegant row of engineers' houses was built (Roughdown Villas Road) and Boxmoor was on the map! Welsh slate for houses came via the canal and the first commuters arrived. ...

Most members of the Boxmoor Residents' Association would still be able to recall characters like 'Bonny' Proctor, the dairyman, whose cows used to wander daily along St. John's Road to graze on the Moor. Or 'Waxy Bates', the cobbler, in a bowler hat he had worn for so long it had turned green. Mr. Marshall the chemist made his own patent medicines and kept bees, often leaving the shop to collect a stray swarm. Fred Mansbridge, the jovial baker, delivered bread in a horse and cart; his remaining family still bake bread on premises they have occupied for one hundred years. Charman, the butcher, killed his own prize beef, having walked the animals from the station in style. Many locals remember their schooldays in the old Infants School in Cowper Road with fearful outside toilets that flushed in spasmodic torrents, and the watchful eye of Miss Vigor 'the Tiger'.

The inhabitants today are grateful for the easy access to London by train and for the varied pleasures given by both the extensive common lands and the Grand Union Canal. Although only a mile away from Hemel Hempstead New Town, they still feel a sense of belonging to a 'village'.

Bramfield

The name Bramfield, recorded in the Domesday Book as Brande-felle, is the last of several derivations of the original name. It is a unique little village in a rural setting 3 miles north-west of Hertford, 5 miles north-east of Welwyn Garden City and 9 miles south of Stevenage. It is hard to believe that London is only 24 miles to the south of this peaceful village surrounded by farmland. Bramfield consists of 111 houses and a population of approximately 300.

In the centre there is a village green, surrounded by cottages, some very old, and a small church.

The original church is reputed to have been built during the 11th century and rebuilt early in the 14th century. It lies in the diocese of St. Albans and is recorded as the first living of St. Thomas-a-Becket. The church seats 100 people and has some fine stained glass windows. It is surrounded by a very neatly-kept churchyard and the local people have recently worked 100 tapestry kneelers of various designs.

Next to the church is a 17th-century thatched cottage which was the Church School until 1935, when about 20 children attended. Since then the Hertfordshire County Council has provided transport for the children to attend nearby schools, so in 1937 the school was converted to a shop and Post Office.

On the south side of the village green is a Spring Water Well, 60 ft. deep, in early years the only source of water for the village. This was used until the end of the First World War, a large iron wheel and chains winding up and down two big leather-studded buckets. Four standing water taps were then placed in various positions nearer the cottages.

During 1937 water was piped into every house from a nearby reservoir, the well being reinforced and concreted over for safety. On 2nd June 1953, it was converted into a bus shelter to commemorate the Coronation of H.M. Queen Elizabeth II.

During early years Bramfield was an agricultural community with four farms, but with the changes in farming methods only two now remain. People find alternative work in the nearby towns and factories.

For a small village it has a very nice recreation field on which stands the Village Hall.

The inhabitants of the village worked very hard organising fêtes, pig-roasts and other events, to raise enough money to build this hall in 1970 and it is much used by many local organisations.

Braughing

Braughing (pronounced Braffing) is very much a village of the present but its quiet corners and main street have many charming old buildings and a sense of history.

There has been a settlement here since Roman times and what is now the B1368 Newmarket road has seen everything from chariots and stage coaches to the modern cars, which at peak times rush commuters along so fast it is doubtful if they ever notice Braughing at all. The names of several houses on this stretch of road show that once they were inns catering to the needs of travellers in times when getting from place to place was a much slower business. The Bird in Hand, The Bell, now the Post Office, the Black Bull at Dassels, also the Chestnuts and the Gables, were all hostelries in days gone by, beer being brewed locally at the Maltings, which are now cottage dwellings, or sometimes it was made behind the inns themselves.

Older residents can remember when the row of houses next to the Post Office, recently a garage, was a blacksmiths and wheel-wrights, and when Green Lane really was a green cart-track through the fields.

Once there were a lot of shops. Now only three remain, one of them White's butchers, where the famous Braughing sausages are made, the Post Office general store, and the little greengrocers, whose owner, a villager born and bred, can tell you many tales of Braughing in days gone by.

Of course, Braughing has its ghosts. A Grey Lady has been seen by a resident alive today. He actually stopped to offer her a lift in his car, only to find she had vanished. A Friar is supposed to walk in Friars Road – where else? – and five ghostly monks doing penance for a misdeed long ago haunt the lower end of Upp Hall Lane, known as Horse Cross. This name has been changed from Whore's Cross, named for the unhappy Ann Boleyn. There is also reputed to be 'something nasty' at the sewer farm on the Dassels road, where a man with some illgotten money came to a sticky end – in pre-sewer days.

If you happen to be passing through the village on 2nd October at approximately 4 o'clock, you may wonder why there is a small gathering of children complete with a broom each at the top of Fleece Lane and in the distance the tolling of the church funeral bell. It is because it is Old Man's Day.

Over 400 years ago a widower named Matthew Wall became ill and appeared to die. Funeral arrangements were made and on the day of the burial, 2nd October, the cortege progressed down Fleece Lane. One of the pall bearers slipped on some wet leaves and the coffin fell to the ground. Faint noises were heard to come from inside the coffin, the lid was prised open and the supposedly dead Matthew Wall sat up and looked around in amazement. Matthew recovered from his illness and shock, remarried and raised a family.

When he died his will, dated 1595, contained certain requests, one of which was a shilling for a poor man to sweep Fleece Lane from his house to the church gate and a shilling for the tolling of the funeral bell. Now every 2nd October the funeral bell is tolled, the lane is swept by the village children and prayers are said at his grave. In the evening the bells are rung out to commemorate the happy event which followed Matthew Wall's unusual experience!

Brent Pelham

About 970 yards north-west of Brent Pelham church lies a moat enclosing a mound, circular in form, which arises from the open surface of the surrounding field to about 6 feet, but its apex, for about 20 feet in width, is rather flat. There appears to be an indication of an attempt at excavation on this mound, only nothing of such excavation has been recorded. Most likely the mound was formed in early British or Roman times, as a burial place for an important chief or high official.

The situation of the tumuli rather points to it being of Celtic period, as no Roman road is supposed to have existed anywhere in the immediate vicinity or within a radius of two miles, although around the district Roman pottery has been dug up.

At Brent Pelham Hall there is a small collection of Roman pottery consisting of many ornamental fragments of vessels, cinerary urns and one very fine water bottle, together with horse shoes, coins and other objects indicating the presence of Romans in the district.

There is evidence of many moated properties in this area, e.g. Beeches, Shonks and Brent Pelham Hall.

Near the South Gate of the church stands the original stocks and whipping post.

Village amenities of the 19th century consisted of a wheelwright and blacksmith, two grocers, a carpenter, shoemaker, bricklayer, undertaker and a draper. Brent Pelham has its own school built in 1860 for 60 children, although the average attendance was only 25. There was also a police station, a club room and village hall, a cricket club and the local pub, the Black Horse. Sadly all that remains of these amenities today is a general store and Post Office, the Village Hall and the Black Horse.

Brickendon ✑

Brickendon was for centuries the property of Waltham Abbey, a few miles to the south. This came about in 1062, when King Harold, so soon to die at the Battle of Hastings, confirmed his foundation of the Abbey and his granting to it of eighteen manors, including Brickendon. The estate was farmed by the monks – perhaps Brickendonbury was the site of an abbey grange and there was a farm at Monks Green – but there was no church: villagers had to worship at All Saints, Hertford, which also belonged to the abbey. In 1539, Henry VIII dissolved the monastery and the manor of Brickendon was bought by Thomas Knighton of Bayford, so the parishes were linked for a time.

The present Brickendonbury House was built on a moated site (where, incidentally, Roman coins and pottery have been found) in the early 18th century by the Clarke family and later passed to the Morgan family, who gave their name to the magnificent avenue of trees, nearly three-quarters of a mile in length, known as Morgan's Walk, by which the house is approached on the Hertford side. Considerable additions and alterations were made by the Pearson family in the 19th century.

The village itself grew up about a mile and a half to the south of the mansion, mainly around a large green, on which there are five oaks, each planted to commemorate jubilees or coronations of five sovereigns from Queen Victoria to our present Queen. There is a village hall, Fanshaws Room, once a barn belonging to Fanshaws Farm. There is also a public house, the 'Farmers Boy', near the green, behind which lies the newer part of the village. The parish is known as Brickendon Liberty, because Henry II in about 1184 gave to the ancient manor liberty or freedom from certain taxes.

The local industry in both parishes is mainly farming, though there are also the research activities of various organisations on some of the larger estates, such as the ecology and astronomy centres of the Hatfield Polytechnic at Bayfordbury, the laboratories of the Malaysian Rubber Producers Research Association at Brickendonbury and the headquarters of the Institute of the Motor Industry at Fanshaws. Also, Bayford Station, situated midway between the two villages, affords frequent train services to London, covenient for commuters to the City and West End (and is also used by weekend hikers from London, who often favour the area as a starting point for country rambles).

Bricket Wood 🌿

Bricket Wood is a small village of approximately 5000 inhabitants and is situated in Hertfordshire equidistant from St. Albans, Watford and Radlett. Hansted's, part of Bricket Wood (or Bryghteyght as it was known in 1539), is named in the Domesday Book. Hansted's is now known as the *C.E.G.B.* Management and Staff Training College but was formerly the home and estate of Lord David and Lady Yule. Lady Yule kept and bred thoroughbred Arabian Stallions for racing and had her own siding and horse box at the railway station for her own carriage. She was at one time reputed to be the richest woman in England. Lord David is buried on the estate in a tomb which also encloses the empty urn, which was used to scatter Lady Yule's ashes in Scotland.

Naturist Camps have long been established in Bricket Wood, to such an extent that in the 1920s and 1930s there were eight flourishing Nudist Colonies. Club members ate the wild fruit and nuts from the woods and held health classes.

The railway line was cut through the wood and commonland between St. Albans and Watford in the 1850s. Although just a halt at first, public demand saw the station open at Bricket Wood in 1862, the line became a double track after 1911, when a second platform was also built. At about this time outings were very popular from London Sunday Schools to the Bricket Wood Fairgrounds, which faced each other across the green. Gray's Fair started in 1889, Christmas's began in the 1900s. Adult outings also enjoyed the fairground atmosphere and especially the afternoon teas which rounded off the day out, as experienced by a ladies' outing from the Straw Factory at Luton. The steam trains from London came straight through to Bricket Wood, and unloaded sometimes as many as eight excursion trains in a day for the 'trip to the fair'. On the way back from the fair the Sunday School children could buy bunches of flowers from the cottages they passed to take home as a gift for mother. The guard on the train always kept an eye open for stragglers and ensured that they caught the train.

At about this time the rest of the village consisted mainly of a few bungalows, homesteads, and prefabricated dwellings – no made-up roads, just country lanes, cinder tracks and rough paths with many pot-holes to trap the unwary traveller. Fresh food was brought into the village by tradesmen from Radlett – meat, fish, vegetables and fruit. Fresh milk was delivered daily in churns by two women. The village had a resident doctor whose surgery was in Bucknalls Drive. (In the 1980s we have a Doctors' Practice at St. Lukes Church Hall, a weekly Baby Clinic and a Dental Practice.)

Fifty years ago no sewage system was available, so every garden had its own cess-pit. Also in the garden was a pump for fresh spring water, which was obtained from the well which sometimes had to be sunk to a depth of 110 feet.

In 1956 the first housing estate was built to house the aircraft workers and their families from Handley Page at Radlett. The Post Office was also a general stores at this time. However there were three other stores in the village, and the bakery still provides hot bread and fresh cakes and buns to this day.

Further building projects began in the late 1950s and several parades of shops were built over the next few years. The scenic beauty of the Railway Station has resulted in several films being made there, amongst them *Queen Victoria* starring the late Anna Neagle.

In the 1980s Bricket Wood is a very busy and interesting community with many and varied organizations thriving including W.I., Brownies, Guides, Cubs, Scouts, Darby and Joan, Ratepayers' Association, Art Club, Horticultural Club, Copper Beech Club, Cricket Club, Bricket Wood Society. The Society collects every item possible relating to the history and interest of Bricket Wood. Its second booklet on the village was published in 1985 and copies were sold to many overseas countries.

With the easy access to all parts of the country now possible by Railway and Motorway. Bricket Wood is still a peaceful haven of quiet and solitude, and consequently a much sought-after residential area.

Brookmans Park 🌿

Brookmans Park village lies within the parish of North Mymms and is situated off the Great North Road roughly equidistant from Potters Bar and Hatfield.

To the romantically inclined, Brookmans Park could well have been a contender for the title of a Jane Austen novel, since at the time that she was writing her enduring classics, two very handsome mansions existed here, complete with their wealthy and influential owners. They, in turn, ensured employment for a large number of servants and tradespeople, the latter, such as blacksmiths, bricklayers and carpenters being paid handsomely by direct employment of labour.

One of the houses, Brookmans, was owned by Lord John Somers (1651–1716) who occupied it for the last 15 years of his life. He was one of the most influential men in Britain, having served as Lord Chancellor in the reign of William and Mary. Later, in the 19th century, a newcomer, Robert William Gaussen was in possession of Brookmans for 64 years and included in his initial purchase was the mansion of Gobions, or Gubbins as it was then called. This house stood on the site of More Hall, a medieval house, which is reputed to have been the home of the family of Sir Thomas More.

Gobions was a fine 18th-century building of palatial proportions, situated in what is now an open space for the use of local inhabitants. Sadly, the mansion of Gobions was systematically demolished by Gaussen, for no apparent reason, soon after it came into his possession. Folly Arch, a red brick edifice dating from 1754, is all that remains of the Gobions buildings and was originally known as the Triumphal Arch. It is situated close to the road leading from Little Heath to Brookmans Park and from this arch there existed a tree-lined avenue leading to the Pleasure Gardens which were renowned in their day. 'The Lion's Den', 'The Temple' and the bowling green have all disappeared, leaving only the arch and lake to testify to the existence of Gobions.

In 1891, whilst the Gaussen family were on holiday, the main house at Brookmans was demolished by fire and was never rebuilt. The stables were converted into a dwelling house where the family lived until 1923 and today it serves as the clubhouse for the Brookmans Park golf course.

With the passing of these two great houses, the extensive land originally owned by the Gaussen family was developed and with the arrival of the railway station in 1926, the farmlands and meadows were being replaced with bricks and mortar. The original scheme was to make Brookmans Park into a garden city but the idea was soon abandoned. Development was rapid from the 1930s to 1950s and in the 1981 census it was revealed that approximately 5000 people live here.

Two interesting houses have survived the passage of time. They are situated on the hill in Moffats Lane. One is called Moffats Farm and is the older of the two properties, possibly dating back to the 16th century. It is reputed that a Dr. Thomas Muffett, an entomologist, once lived there and that he wrote the nursery rhyme *Little Miss Muffet* after his little daughter, Patience, had had an encounter with a spider!

The other house, Moffats, of Georgian design, was occupied in later years by Mr. Arthur Wilson Fox, whose father was physician in ordinary to Queen Victoria. His wife was a direct descendant of Sir Thomas More, and like her illustrious forbear, was interested in the social problems of the day and spoke to Women's Institutes on local government. She was also a short story writer, her stories being of 'a high moral tone'!

Broxbourne

Broxbourne has grown from a small village to a large one in the space of 35 years.

The name Broxbourne is derived from the Saxon word 'Broc' or Badger and Bourne, a stream. Even now the Badgers are taken care of by a passage under the new A10 road.

The old Manor House of Baas Hill is said to have belonged to Leofric at the time of the Domesday Book in 1086. The present Manor House, Broxbournebury, was a 16th century house, re-modelled in the 19th century. Here King James I was entertained in 1603. An interesting place on the estate is the old Icehouse, which still has the cellar under the floor where ice was kept for the Manor House. Today Broxbournebury is used as a special school for children with learning difficulties.

Broxbourne church, St. Augustines, was built in the 15th century, although there was a church in Broxbourne earlier, at the time of Edward the Confessor. The font is made of Purbeck Marble. On the wall in the south aisle is a tablet to the memory of John MacAdam, the great improver of British roads.

To the north of Broxbourne, the woodlands are still a joy to walk through, and now have planned walks and pathways.

Buntingford 🐚

Buntingford has a population of about 5000, and is situated where the main Roman road to the North – Ermine Street crosses the river Rib at a ford. It is first mentioned in 1185 in records of land owned by the Knights Templar, and by the Middle Ages was an important market centre and location for judicial enquiries. Henry III, in 1253, granted a market to the manor of Corneybury. Buntingford's first market charter was in 1360, followed by various others granted up to the time of Henry VIII, whose grant of 1542 is still in existence.

Prosperity declined generally with the Black Death of 1348, but returned as trade and travel increased; by the early 17th century Buntingford had a Bridewell, Grammar School and several important inns, such as The George and The Bell. The latter, divided now into two separate establishments by its stableyard arch, is reputed to be haunted by the ghost of a servant girl who smothered her baby.

At the present time there are six public houses although at the turn of the century there were fifteen, many of which had extensive stabling and grazing for horses, and the population was a third of today's!

The first turnpike road in the country authorised by Parliament in 1663 ran through Buntingford, from Wadesmill to the south, north through Royston on to Huntingdon. The turnpike Trustees usually met in The George. Exactly two hundred years later a railway line was opened between Buntingford and St. Margaret's on the Liverpool Street Line. The railway was intended to continue north through Royston to Cambridge, but never progressed, and was one of many which fell to the Beeching axe.

48

Now the wheel is turning full circle; the road which brought trade and prosperity to the town brings the traffic – large lorries which are shaking the old buildings to pieces, cracking the pavements as they ride up over the kerbs in their haste to reach their destinations, not to mention causing alarm and danger to pedestrians. Relief though is at hand, after thirty years of campaigning and promises, work started in January 1986 on a by-pass, a modern traffic innovation which should have as great an effect on Buntingford as Ermine Street did nearly a thousand years ago.

Childwick Green 🐚

As you travel along the main A1081 road towards Harpenden, about 2 miles out of St. Albans, you pass on your left a handsome pair of wrought iron gates and a lodge, obviously the entrance to a large estate. Do not pass by, but turn into the drive for you are entering Childwick Bury and in a quarter of a mile you will come to the hamlet of Childwick Green (pronounced 'Chillick' Green). Linger along the drive in daffodil time for the verges are golden with blooms, backed by woods with trees in green bud and wild cherry in bloom, or linger when the magnificent rhododendrons are a mass of colour, the azaleas aflame and the woods carpeted with bluebells. The drive twists tortuously and the hamlet is seen only after the last bend. From Childwick Green you can walk further along the drive with pasture land and woods on either side towards the manor house of Childwick Bury and on back to St. Albans. The manor of Childwick Bury dates back to Saxon times and in 1077 was called Childewicam.

In the present century the estate was auctioned and bought by Mr. J. B. Joel. In 1940 his son, Mr. Harry (Jim) Joel, inherited and carried on the family tradition of keeping one of the best studs in the country. In 1967 his horse, *Royal Palace*, won the Derby and the 2000 Guineas. *Royal Palace* sired *Dunfermline*, the Queen's dual Classic winner in 1977. The Joel family concerned themselves greatly in the welfare of their tenants and made gifts to the church. The schoolroom was used until about 1925 and re-opened for evacuees during the Second World War. It is now the meeting room and is used by the W.I. The end property of the row of cottages was until 1952 the One Bell public house, it was then converted to a private club for the employees. Finally the Joel

EB

family sold the estate to a property company, Broadlands, who then auctioned it in 1978 through J. D. Wood, selling most of the farmland and the houses as separate lots. The houses have been made into very attractive homes, maintaining the beauty of Childwick Green. Mr. Joel kept the stud and still lives at Stud House and he also retained some houses for his working and retired staff. The mansion was sold privately to Mr. Stanley Kubrick, the film director. It is a very fine house dating back to 1666 with additions made by later owners.

Chipperfield

The village of Chipperfield lies in the Manor of Kings Langley, with the towns of Hemel Hempstead to the north and Watford to the south.

The earliest record relating to Chipperfield was in 1316, when Edward II bequeathed 'the Manor House of Langley the closes adjoining together with the vesture of Chipperfieldwode' to the Dominican Brothers.

With the Dissolution of the Monasteries in the 16th century, Chipperfield was no longer the hunting ground for Kings and Queens. The friars no longer visited their fish pool where they would fish and meditate. The Pool, in later times called the Apostles Pond is surrounded by 12 lime trees, planted about 1714. These are supposed to represent the 12 Apostles, hence the name of the Pool. These have recently been lopped and 12 new trees planted to take their place when they eventually die.

Grouped around the woods are great sweet chestnuts, brought over by the Crusaders. They are planted now in threes and singly. The oldest surviving tree is 750 years old, and is near the fish pool.

Starting from the west end of the Common was a wooden windmill on the hill where the ground fell away and the strong south-west wind caught the sails. The Millhouse close by had a bakery where loaves were sold from the window. Across the Common the old School Barn and the old house Mahagony Hall stands. This at one time was the old school. Between the Windmill and the Common crossroads on which stand the Two Brewers Inn were two well-used cock pits. Chipperfield is one of the last places in England where cock fighting was known.

The Two Brewers Inn is 16th century and originally consisted of a shop on the corner, the pub and the Schoolmaster's house. The Pub was a well known venue for the Boxing fraternity. Facing the Cricket ground, it was also the meeting place for Cricketers, who would come down from London and elsewhere, playing in tall hats. There were matches of more than one day when tents were erected against the churchyard wall and the Two Brewers supplied meals there and barrels of beer.

From *Notes on old Chipperfield* published during the 1950s it is noted that beadwork and straw plaiting were the cottage industries of the village, the work being taken to Hemel Hempstead for sale. The work was done on strips of net 2 or 3 inches wide, with very fine needles and black and white beads and coloured spangles.

Water in the summer was a problem and it is recorded that water from the Pool was indeed the source for the village together with wells in some cottage gardens, and would be carried by the bucketful to the Manor House.

The Village Hall which is opposite the Parish Church is managed by a committee composed of representatives from the various village organisations. In recent years the hall has been modernised with the help of grants from local Authorities and now is a very popular venue for family events as well as fund raising projects and other meetings.

In spite of its close proximity to the county town of Watford and the motorways nearby, Chipperfield has managed to retain its character as a typical English Village.

Chipping Barnet ✒

Chipping Barnet derives its name from the privilege granted to the monks of St. Albans of holding a market there, the word 'cheap' signifying a market. Although Barnet became part of the enlarged G.L.C. in 1964, the Post Office in its wisdom retained the identity of Barnet as a Hertfordshire town. Barnet Hill quite dramatically slams the door on London, due to the position of the parish church at the top of the quite considerable slope. Quite literally the church divides the road, the north-west branch, Wood Street, linking up eventually with Watling Street, the north-east branch being Barnet High Street, which becomes the Great North Road, taking the historic route to York.

At the end of the High Street is Hadley Green, where on a misty Easter Sunday in 1471, Edward IV defeated Warwick the King-maker who was killed in the battle. There is a memorial obelisk to mark the site and an imaginative council has named roads nearby after the families of that struggle – King Edward, Warwick, Woodville, Clifford, Mowbray to name some of them.

Barnet Horse Fair, held by right of a charter from Queen Elizabeth I during the first week in September, is one of the major venues for trading in Welsh horses and ponies. Even in the 1950s there was quite a lot of activity in the Underhill area with horses being put through their paces on open ground near the road, but the danger from heavy traffic and the building of new council housing has forced the dealers to a field further from the main road. There used to be a pleasure fair at the same time, and there were two swing boats that were steam driven, the heap of coal dumped beside them.

The Barnet Physic Well stands on a small triangle of grass near the bottom of Wellhouse Lane, all that is left of Barnet Common, which was enclosed during the 18th century. The well, whose purgative water had a reputation equal to that of Tunbridge and Epsom, was visited by Samuel Pepys, and indeed for several decades, Barnet had a reputation as a spa. Also on the common was a racecourse which finally disappeared with the arrival of the railway in 1871.

Until the 1950s and 60s, Barnet possessed a fine collection of family-owned shops. There were two ladies' outfitters, with deep entrances and 'walk-round' island windows. The Star tavern had a working blacksmith in its yard, Mr. Hentall had a cycle shop and another member of the family an ironmongers. The first floor of another draper's shop was a former Assembly Room and the four nicely rounded windows (rebuilt) look across the traffic to the church. Happily a jewellery shop with its black and gold fascia board is still run by Mr. Kelsey, and the dignified portal of the Barnet Press with its clock is a reminder of the past. Waitrose Supermarket is on the site of the former Barnet Cinema, Boots modern shop replaces the former building which had a fine porch supported by pillars from the pavement.

Of the many inns in Barnet, the Mitre still has a fine timbered archway into the yard, a reminder of the days when Barnet was an important coaching station.

Chorleywood

Chorleywood is in the south west corner of Hertfordshire; south of the A404 between Amersham in Buckinghamshire and Rickmansworth in Hertfordshire. It is in the Green Belt (jealously guarded) with farm land, woods and parks. In the older part of the village there are buildings of Tudor origin, King John's Farm where William Penn was married and where he attended services in the Manor House then called the Quakers Meeting House; there are Tudor Cottages in Chorleywood Bottom and The Retreat across the road known as Youngs Farm, the home of the late Robert Turney who was considered an authority on the History of Chorleywood. He was always willing to discuss his beloved Chorleywood. There are many old residents whose first school was the Church of England School on the Common and their ancestors built the flint cottages which stand side-by-side with the new houses and flats.

The Turnpike was the only real road in Chorleywood and was surfaced in 1914 to provide easier transit for the Marquis of Salisbury by carriage on his way from Hatfield House to the Spa in

Bath. It was then referred to as the 'Gout Road'! Charges were made at the Toll Cottage at the Gate Inn and there used to be a sign outside the Inn reading:

'This Gate hangs well
It hinders none
Refresh and pay
And travel on'

The other ways were cart tracks and footpaths.

The Common – the glory of Chorleywood – covers about 200 acres, colourful in all seasons. Gorse blooms even in winter, bullrushes can be seen by the ponds. Always welcome is the green holly, the heather and of course the blackberries and wild strawberries.There are now four ponds which were carefully constructed and today depend on refills from the rain. These were originally for the watering of cattle and sheep and a welcome sight to the Drovers taking their animals to market. Rabbits are again to be seen and the grey squirrel is familar even in gardens. Foxes are around and can be heard barking at night. Some badger setts are known.

Chorleywood is a very pleasant and friendly place within easy reach of the M25. This has made it attractive for those engaged in professional work, commerce, radio, television, films and theatre. It is within reasonable distance of London Airport on the M25 and there is a train service reaching London in 40 minutes on the Metropolitan Line and British Rail.

Clothall

The tiny village stands enfolded in chalk and clay hills invisible save for its flint rubble church with its squat tower built to withstand the east wind sweeping up from the cold open lands of Clothall Common.

Besides a church the village had all else needful – several farms, a beerhouse, village hall, school, almshouses, and a never-run-dry spring.

Times have changed. The Barley Mow is licensed no longer, the children are 'bussed' to school in Baldock. One almshouse has been sold to provide for the improvement of the other and we now have piped water. There are probably fewer houses in the village now than a hundred years ago but we still have some fine old buildings. There is the former Rectory where parsons of noble but penurious ancestry played the squire, in an early Georgian mansion and across the lane stands a Queen Anne farmhouse in patched red brick. A beautiful Elizabethan farmhouse atop a high ridge looks across to a sister hill where yet another farmhouse marks the site of the Great House of Quickswood where the Earls of Salisbury kept their mistresses.

Times change again. Suddenly a mushroom development sprang up on Clothall Common where no hardy soul has lived since the Romans. Their successors found the abandoned wells and called it 'Walls'.

The village is smaller now and the community less close knit but we still have our church albeit in plurality with three larger villages. Every year at midsummer we fill a barn with friends from the village and its surroundings, regale them with unpretentious wines and a marvellous selection of cheeses, painlessly extract their money and send them home replete on the one night of the year when we are on the map.

Cockernhoe

·The small village of Cockernhoe lies just two and a half miles from the centre of Luton and eight miles from Hitchin. Once just a handful of estate cottages (from the nearby Putteridge estate) nestling round the two village greens Cockernhoe Green and Mangrove Green, and three working farms, the village is now being threatened by the steadily expanding town of Luton. However it lies just across the border in Hertfordshire and at present is separated from the new housing estates by a row of fields.

To the north of the village the narrow roads rise and fall, twist and turn through some of the most beautiful countryside in Hertfordshire. The village now has just one working farm and a gamekeeper and shoot. The village pub lies on the edge of Mangrove Green.

The village school, built in 1881 has around fifty children — infant and junior. In the past most of the men in the village worked on the land and many of the women made or trimmed hats. The motor industry and Luton Airport now offer work to many of the villagers and only a few men are employed on the land but quite a few are employed by a local agricultural machine specialist. Ladies still trim hats both in Luton and their own homes.

Codicote 🌿

Cudda's Cot boasted a population of sixteen villeins, one Frenchman, four serfs and three cottars. There were two mills, pastures and woodland enough to feed two hundred swine. These facts are recorded in the Domesday Book.

Today, Codicote is a sprawl of relatively new housing estates with a largely commuting population, yet only 150 years ago Codicote was a very different place.

Lying just north of Welwyn on the Hitchin road, it was a close-knit, mainly self-supporting community with almost every skill needed for survival within its parish boundary. Two forges, one of which was operated by a female farrier called Elizabeth Cain (who continued at the anvil until well into her nineties) two wheelwrights, a coach trimmer and a saddler took care of travellers.

There was a bakehouse where bread was baked for the villagers and the surrounding hamlets, and where the women could bake their own bread or maybe a Christmas goose for a small payment.

A chimney-sweep, a plumber, builder, hurdle maker and even an undertaker were all available. The day to day necessities were catered for by a draper, grocer, shoemaker, cobbler and a butcher who slaughtered on the premises. There was even a travelling fishmonger. The village was well served by the licensed trade. There were five inns and as many ale-houses. Many of these have disappeared, having been changed to residential use.

The oldest documented licensed premises in Hertfordshire is in Codicote. This is the George and Dragon, it is now a Chinese restaurant. Records show that it existed in 1279. It was rebuilt in 1550 being known as the Greyhound for a time. Pilgrims on their way to worship at the shrine of St. Alban used it, and in later years drovers on their way to the London markets pasturing their herds in nearby fields.

There was a workhouse within the churchyard wall, a poorhouse, a pound, a lock-up for the local petty criminals and stocks on the 'Hill', an open space opposite the George.

Codicote's church school in Bury Lane was established in 1857, some years before the surrounding villages could boast such an achievement. Sadly, this has disappeared under yet another housing development.

The Parish Church of St. James is the oldest building in the village dating from the 12th century, though it has been restored several times.

The Bury is a fine 17th century manor house which in the last decade was acquired by the Johnny Johnson Trust and now provides sheltered housing for pensioners in purpose-built extensions and bungalows.

Codicote Lodge, another manor house, stands on the site of an Elizabethan manor called Stagenhoe Hall which was demolished around 1800. The Node, up to the beginning of the 19th century, was an ordinary farmhouse, but in 1811 it changed hands and a series of enlargements resulted in it becoming one of the most important houses in the parish. Buried in the churchyard are two maids who were employed at the Node, who were found to have suffocated in their beds from the fumes from a pan of charcoal they had taken to warm their bedroom. Codicote's first census in 1801 shows a population of 584, fifty years later it had jumped to 1227. Today it is in excess of 3000 and rising.

We in the 20th century might feel that the village was a more interesting and picturesque place in those days, but the inhabitants of 'picturesque' Codicote would undoubtedly have preferred the modern village. After all, there have been no outbreaks of cholera or smallpox to decimate the population, infant mortality is a thing of the past, no one starves because they can't find work, and we don't have to carry our water from one of the two village pumps.

Colliers End

Colliers End is situated just to the south of a Roman crossroads, where the minor road from Verulamium crossed Ermine Street on the way to Camulodunum (Colchester). There may have been a few small buildings here and a wooden bridge over the stream just to the south of the village, near Labdens. This name is derived from the 14th century name Lapdenbrigge, meaning the bridge in the valley. A causeway was built at the beginning of the 19th century and the stream was run through a tunnel.

Nicholas le Colyere gave his name to the village, according to the Assize Rolls of 1278 and by 1526 the place was called Colyersend, with end meaning a hamlet. The inhabitants earned their livelihoods from agriculture with its associated crafts and from the important road traffic on what was the old North Road. At Wadesmill, the country's first turnpike was built and the road from London to Cambridge was the first to have milestones. At Colliers End there was a weighbridge, according to the 1840 tithe map that shows the Weighbridge House on the site of the old army camp. Not only corn but coal was carried through the village by horse-drawn wagons between the canals leading to Cambridge and the river Lee from Ware to London. The coaches passed through Colliers End, stopping at Puckeridge, as Samuel Pepys recorded in his diary, but the other traffic must have helped to keep the village inns in business. The oldest of these is the Lamb and Flag or Holy Lamb as it was called until about 1840 when the building previous to the present one was built. The Holy Lamb was the symbol of the Crusaders and the Knights of St. John are known to have been active around Standon. The tenant around 1840 was Thomas Bangs who might have been related to Phoebe Bangs who, according to the 1890 Kelly's Directory, kept the Model Guest House in Ware's Kibes Lane.

Across the road from the Lamb and Flag is an old timber-framed house now called Cobwebs that was formerly the Wagon and Horses. Farther north, there was the Red, White and Blue, now Barnacres and across the road, The Plough, that has been replaced by two new houses. The Fox and Hounds, at the old Roman crossroads, is now a private dwelling but the pub name has been retained.

Being one of the few villages in East Herts without a speed limit below 60 m.p.h., Colliers End is looking forward to being by-passed. In spite of the divisive effect of the constant traffic, there are some social activities in the village such as fun days, rummage sales, discos and the fortnightly visit of the mobile library gives villagers a reason to meet for coffee in the hall. Like most small villages it is no longer a self-contained unit but the church, hall and pub are still meeting places for the inhabitants.

Colney Heath ✍

Colney Heath village lies just to the east of St. Albans, snuggling into a corner of the huge triangle created by the A405, the A1 and the A6. The M25 has an interchange less than two miles away.

The Parish of Colney Heath, although centred on the village itself, stretches out to include the delightful hamlets of Tyttenhanger, Smallford, Sleapshyde and Wilkins Green, all of which, in common with the other areas that make up the parish, have fine examples of extremely old cottages or houses, as well as representative buildings of every decade this century.

The river Colne, which also gives its name to London Colney and Colney Street, is small but extremely pretty as it babbles through Colney Heath, although it can become a raging torrent during long spells of wet or snowy weather. It is joined by the Ellenbrook on the southern side of the heath, and is home to greedy herons and gorgeous kingfishers.

The heath itself is the last remnant of the old manorial lands of Tyttenhanger, owned by the Abbey until the Dissolution of the Monasteries. It is a beautiful natural area which, although it supports a number of comparatively rare plants, is smaller and less colourful (albeit safer!) today than in the past, when it was the haunt of not-so-rare footpads and highwaymen, and the location for cock fighting and prize fights.

The pubs of the parish are still linked together by old footpaths, which must tell us something about our ancestors! Some bear rustic names – The Crooked Billet and two called The Plough; The Barley Mow probably did a bit of home brewing, whilst The Queens Head seems to attest a certain loyalty to the Crown. The Horseshoes and The Cock were probably named after the game of horseshoes and the earlier-mentioned cock fights respectively. The Chalkdrawers Arms is a reminder that chalk was drawn (or dug) locally.

There was once a tollgate in the village, and there is still a coal post to be seen in Coursers Road. These coal posts marked not only the boundary of the Metropolitan area for delivering coal, but also the limit of Metropolitan Police authority. It was very easy, therefore, for law breakers to leg it across the boundary to the appropriate side and thumb their noses with impunity (and dirty hands, no doubt) at the representatives of whichever law was after them. This little benefit no longer applies, needless to say!

Today the Parish and village are much more law-abiding, and are united with community activities such as the Town Twinning Association, the twin being Boissy in France. The Scouts and Guides, the Youth Club, a football team, the P.T.A. and, of course, the W.I. are some of the activities which go on. An excellent Parish magazine is published quarterly and distributed to every house free of charge, and keeps everyone in touch with what is going on. An active Parish Council meets regularly, and anyone may attend their meetings.

There is a village carnival every year now, into which the Women's Institute throw themselves with enthusiasm, a Produce Show which they organise, and in 1985 a 'Bed or Bath Race' for charity won the ladies an award for the best turned-out team! They *were* magnificent, sporting 'bathing belle' costumes and propelling their smallest and lightest member in a handsome streamlined bath. They may have been last, competing as they were with some brawny teams from the local hostelries, but they certainly brought up the rear in style!

Cuffley 🐚

Way back in time the site of Cuffley was an area of natural mineral springs considered to be beneficial to health and visited by jaded royal parties to partake of these waters. Older residents will remember one such water meadow opposite the first shops in Cuffley's main thoroughfare Station Road and the boggy expanse of fields alongside our local brook. Other evidence of these wells is provided by names of roads such as 'Kingswell Ride', 'King James Avenue' and our local farm 'Wells Farm'. However, these springs have now been mostly channelled away and only a few are visible after a very sudden rain storm.

Around about the time that the village was a kind of spa area the then open grass and woodland was part of the Chace used for hunting the deer and other wild animals by royal parties from the City of London.

Cuffley, as most inhabitants now know it, really started to flourish as a village when a railway, then the Great Northern, extended its tracks from Enfield in Middlesex to Hertford. After

HILDA WALLER JONES.

much effort Cuffley Viaduct, clearly seen from a number of roads into the village, was finally completed and Cuffley station came into use.

Our most noteworthy claim to fame came in World War One with the shooting down of a German Zeppelin on to fields adjacent to Plough Hill by a certain Captain Leefe Robinson, a memorial to whom still stands on a corner of East Ridgeway.

This incident of course was seen in the sky for miles around and resulted in hordes of sightseers and souvenir hunters converging on the tiny and in those days quite insignificant Cuffley via the railway, which the Great Northern had taken no further than the Cuffley halt for the duration, with a view to picking up bits of the 'Zepp' as it was quickly named to make into brooches, fobs and other commemorative pieces. My father was one of these and acquired for himself a piece of metal which, being somewhat of a craftsman he fashioned into a fob which hung on his watch chain thereafter.

Having a railway station on a line into town, Cuffley was a prime target, between the Wars, for private development of properties, mainly bungalows at first as these were thought to be more suited to the clay soil of the district, which was very inclined to slippage and, indeed still is under certain conditions.

However, present day building techniques have made it possible to utilise almost any terrain and Cuffley now has various kinds of development and is a modern thriving village.

At the start of World War Two Cuffley was a reception area for children from London and a number of older members of our community will remember these little lonely evacuees dumped in the village by harassed officials.

Most of our working population are, at the present time, commuters to the City but we do have industry in Cuffley. One of the country's largest supermarkets has a sizeable depot here, we have a firm of timber merchants and a very well-known double glazing company.

One of the most enjoyable aspects of our village is that although we, in this corner of Hertfordshire, are very near the busy industrial heart of London, we are surrounded by the loveliest and most productive countryside. Close to the most modern of motorways – the M25 – we nevertheless have some of the oldest woodland in the country; the Great Wood and Home Wood, as well as many open country walks and rides.

Datchworth ✒

Said to be 'the most haunted village in Hertfordshire'. Certainly there are records of characters considered to have practised the art of witchcraft, some of them leaving their mark in place names about the parish. Some local people even today claim supernatural presences in old houses or lanes.

It is a scattered parish, comprising a number of 'Greens', indicating the clearance and cultivation of woodland after Domesday records were made in 1087. All Saints Church stands at the highest point, and is visible from several miles around. It is believed a church stood on the site before the Norman conquest. Parts are of Norman origin, constructed of flint rubble and stone from local fields, most likely built by local labour. It is small and unpretentious.

Downhill to the south we come to the main crossroads. This is a busy corner, with our general stores and 17th-century Post Office and two public houses nearby. From here a Roman road runs along the south side of Datchworth Green, thought to have been an older track resurfaced, bordered by fine oaks and ashes. At the far corner it reaches 'Hopkyns Hoo', a charming thatched cottage built as a farmhouse in 1570. Three old green lanes converge here. The green itself is a favourite spot for visiting cricket teams and their families, and for the June fête, a lively gathering of friends far and near to join in the traditional junketing. Along the main road across the green the pink and white cherry trees are a lovely sight in spring blossom and a bonus in the red and gold of early autumn foliage.

At the east end of the Green stands the whipping post, a reminder of the days when vagrants unwilling to work in the parish suffered a whipping. It was last known to be used on 27th July 1665, when two vagabonds were publicly flogged. Both stocks and cage stood near the whipping post, but no trace remains of either, and the stocks were said to be 'removed by local inhabitants' in February 1899. In the 18th century a notorious murderer and robber, Walter Clibbon, was shot and killed, a post to mark the spot standing on the brow of the hill to the south, near Bulls Green.

Datchworth is mentioned in the Domesday Book and is also referred to in the Diary of Carrington of Bramfield, Chief Constable and Tax Collector at the end of the 16th century. A comprehensive history of the village was published in 1984 by the Parish Council.

Digswell 🦢

Probably the outstanding landmark in Digswell is the railway viaduct. The Great Northern Railway employed a leading railway contractor, Thomas Brassey, to build the viaduct designed by William Cubitt, the railway's chief engineer, on the lines of a Roman aqueduct. Started in the late 1840s it took 2 years to build, which is quite a remarkable achievement considering it is approximately 1560 ft. long, 100 ft. high from road to railway track and has 40 arches, each with a 30 ft. span. All bricks were manufactured on site where the workmen lived. The first train crossed on 8th August 1850 and today regular traffic is carried from Kings Cross to Edinburgh.

When travelling over the viaduct passengers can look down on to Digswell Lake. Digswell Lake, a small area of woodland and ornamental parkland of about 17½ acres, was once part of the grounds of a large house. The area was bought from The New Towns Commission in 1984 by Digswell Lake Society. The area is maintained regularly by members of the Society who believe the area is worth keeping, not only for its beauty but for the peace and quiet both to visitors and wildlife.

St. John's Church, Digswell, is nearly 800 years old. A church stood on the site at the time of the Norman conquest and today remains of the 12th-century walls may still be seen enclosing the Lady Chapel. The piscina by the high altar may also date from this time. When Digswell prospered in the 13th century, due to the annual fair the church was enlarged when an arcade of 2 bays was inserted in the north wall as well as the north aisle being built.

Sir John Peryent was responsible for the next addition, a chantry chapel built at the east end of the north aisle, and it was completed by 1439. In the 16th century 2 extensions were made to the church, a tower (c 1510) built on to the west end and chantry chapel, then extended to meet the east wall of the chancel. In the 17th century a south porch was erected but is no longer there as this was demolished in the early 1960s when the church was considerably enlarged to accommodate the growth of Welwyn Garden City.

Inside the church are a number of brasses which attract a lot of interest. Those in the best condition are of Sir John Peryent and his Lady who died in 1432 and 1415 respectively. Sir John is depicted in full plate armour of the period and is known to have been Esquire to 3 Kings, pennon bearer to Richard II and Master of Horse to Joan of Navarre, second queen of Henry IV. Lady Joan Peryent was Chief Lady in Waiting to the same Queen and a brass rubbing of her was once used on a British postage stamp.

Flamstead 🦢

Until 20 years ago Flamstead was a small village surrounded by many farms. Most of the men were farm workers while the women and children supplemented the modest wages by plaiting straw for the hat trade in Luton, walking to Luton regularly to deliver their work to the various factories. However, 1965 saw great changes in the village with the development of 4 small estates. The village at present has 500 dwellings and building is restricted to in-filling.

Despite the modern development the centre of the village has changed little and still retains its character. In the High Street are many attractive half timbered and flint cottages. The oldest buildings in the village are the Alms Houses, Saunders Row, built in 1669 founded originally by the Sebright family of Beechwood Park, benefactors to Flamstead for many centuries. The Blacksmith's Cottage and shop is now a private house and there are many attractively converted old farm cottages to be seen in Trowley Bottom.

The village is dominated by its church – St. Leonard's, standing in a large churchyard, whose 'Hertfordshire spike' can be seen on the skyline when approaching the village. The church dates from the 12th century, the first known vicar being Thomas de Bassingham appointed 1223. The tower contains six bells. Five bear the inscription 'Chandles made me, 1664', the sixth bell is inscribed 'John Waylett London, fecit 1729'. The church has reputedly one of the best medieval wall paintings in Hertfordshire. It was discovered in 1929 under layers of plaster and depicts St. Christopher, Christ in Glory, and details of the Last Supper. One of the original consecration crosses has also been uncovered. Another point of interest are the figures on the chancel screen carved in Oberammergau. Three well-worn gravestones can be found in the churchyard bearing the skull and crossbones showing that the village was visited by the Plague in 1604.

Today Flamstead, because of its situation still maintains a tranquil village atmosphere. But conversely because of its easy access to the M1 many residents commute to London and other far flung places. Although only a short distance from Luton Airport, we are happily not too bothered by flights over the village. We are well blessed with Public Houses and have the Blackbirds and Spotted Dog in the village centre, the Rose and Crown in Trowley Bottom and The Waggon and Horses a short walk down the hill to Watling Street. They all attract many visitors to the village. We are fortunate in having two shops: C. Merrit the Butcher, and the Village Stores and Post Office, both are centres for socialising and village chat.

Flamstead End 🦢

Flamstead End is a part of the town of Cheshunt, West Cheshunt, to be exact. Therefore it has no council of its own, but is controlled by Broxbourne Council, which covers quite a large area of Hertfordshire. Up to about 1930 Flamstead End really was a village, much of it was in the so-called Green Belt area, which should not be built on. Nurseries, or greenhouses covered a large part of the land. Tomatoes, cucumbers, carnations and roses were grown, and it was a joy to see the greenhouses full of vines and flowers in spring and summer. On many occasions in the past roses grown at Flamstead End were supplied for the Queen's bouquet. The Lea Valley, under which Flamstead End comes, had an excellent name in the large vegetable markets of the big cities such as London. After World War II many Italians emigrated to this area, they had been used to rearing such plants in their warmer climes, and they worked hard for little pay with great success.

Now many of the greenhouses have gone, and only a few remain. The whole trade is carried on elsewhere, and houses have been built on the land. The Italians seem to have dispersed themselves: there are a few families still left who are now part and parcel of Cheshunt. Flamstead End itself is quite rolling countryside and there are plenty of lovely walks through woods, and also the beautiful area of Cheshunt Park. At the turn of the century, this was a large attractive residence in its own grounds of about 600 acres, owned by four sisters, the Misses Debenham. None of them ever married, and they all lived to be a great age: during their lives they cared for the house and gardens, but it was not open to the public. On their deaths part was sold to Broxbourne Council, the house itself was pulled down as it was, by this time, in a bad state of repair. There is now an 18-hole golf course in the grounds, which is extremely popular in the district as ordinary members of the public can play there, as well as members of the club itself. There is a lake in the grounds, also a golf house and cafe, and many people visit during weekends and holidays in the summertime.

So, Flamstead End is virtually in the country, but it is also part of Cheshunt, and Cheshunt, one would say, is a small town about thirteen miles north of London, in fact it is in the suburbs of London. In 1951 we had a population of approximately 24000 people. By 1973 this had grown to 45000 and in 1985 it is almost 60000, so you will see the district has grown tremendously in the past thirty years. It is mainly residential, but there are a few factories in the industrial area around the British Rail Station.

We cannot end without a mention of Cheshunt Great House, which was in Flamstead End itself, and this dated back to 1450. In 1519 it was purchased by Cardinal Wolsey who kept it till his fall from power, and Elizabeth I used it when passing through from London on her hunting expeditions. There are supposed to be tunnels from the Great House to Waltham Abbey, secret panels and ghosts, but none are verified! It gradually fell into disrepair, and about 20 years ago was accidentally burnt to the ground, a sad day indeed.

Flaunden 🌺

Flaunden village stands some 300 ft. above sea level on the southern border of Hertfordshire.

It started life as a retirement village for workers on the local estates of Lord Chesham of Latimer House. In those days 100 years ago the actual postal address was 'Chesham', Bucks. Hardly any additional building has been done since those days, only a Village Hall and half a dozen council houses; therefore it still retains for most of the day its quiet village atmosphere with the original brick and flintstone cottages radiating out from the central crossroads called 'Crossways'.

This used to be the hub of the village at all times, and recollections of an elderly resident include a visit from a gentleman with a dancing bear, brass bands and some Italians with a barrel organ and monkey.

The original Post Office was in a corner cottage by the church, but later moved into the Crossway along with the village shop and nearby bakery which delivered bread to a very wide radius around. There was also a blacksmith and a butcher's shop situated in aptly-named Hogs Pit Bottom.

Now 50% of the population are commuters, like so many of the villages dotted around London, and there is neither shop, Post Office nor school in the village. The two public houses and village hall are well supported and the hall particularly remains the hub of village life since it was built 15 years ago, supporting play group, W.I., badminton and carpet bowls etc. The old village hall cottage has since been converted to a private residence, as has the village school which is still called 'School House'. Some 80 years ago this school was attended by village children until the age of 8 or 9 years, then began the long 2-mile walk to neighbouring Chenies or Latimer. The school was run by Governesses who lived on the premises and dreaded the periodic visit from the 'Inspector', and the vicar also took an interest in pupils' progress.

Several local farms ring the village and it is still not unusual to be confronted in the main road by the milking herd from central Sharlowes Farm. As long as 80 years ago people were collecting their milk from this farm at an old halfpenny for a full can. In latter days drinking water was obtained from a pump operated by a horse walking round and round to fill the reservoir, but if this failed a water cart was sent up from Latimer and each householder was rationed to two full pails. There were also several wells around the village, some of which exist today in people's gardens. Piped water was finally laid on in about 1903.

Stagg Farm also had a small grocery shop and during the Second World War used to have children down from London for caravan and camping holidays. There now exists on this same place a small residential mobile home site, of which someone's garage used to be the community hall for these London children. Several of the farms still keep pigs commercially, whereas once it was individual householders who used to keep the odd pig fed on scraps and acorns and when these were killed and straw set alight for the subsequent singeing, all the local children thought it was a great event. Also ringing the village were many cherry orchards and a 'cherry-minder' was employed with clapper board to keep the birds from this valuable crop. A local man, Bohmer Goodman, and family were employed for weeks picking the cherries and also walnut, cob or filbert nuts. Many cherry pies were made and sold in the local bakery.

The village boundaries have recently been expanded some half a mile in all directions to include a few more households and now has the status of a Parish Council. It still retains its village atmosphere, helped on by its local W.I.'s annual pancake races etc., a long-standing tradition since the 1960s.

Goffs Oak 🐿️

In the extreme south-east of Hertfordshire is the Borough of Broxbourne and within it and about two miles to the north-west of Cheshunt Parish Church stands our village of Goffs Oak.

There is a widely held local legend that Goff is a derivation of the name Sir Theodore Godfrey, one of William the Conqueror's Barons, who is said to have planted the oak tree here in 1066. It is however known that a Mr. Gough lived here in the early 1800s and when he died it was stated that he was from Goffs Place, Sussex and Goffs Oak. His only surviving relative now lives in Goffs House. Our original oak tree was very large; the trunk was hollow and several people could stand in the cavity. Charles Lamb referred to the tree as 'the old Monster of Cheshunt'. It blew down on 2nd February 1950, but its successor flourishes outside the Goffs Oak Hotel.

Although so near to London, 19 miles by road, this is a rural area, with much attractive and unspoilt scenery of woods, commons and secluded lanes. The land reaches over three hundred feet above sea-level in many places.

The population of our village in 1921 was 1015, today it is probably four times that. The village is centred on the War Memorial, but the original village was probably further to the east, but still roughly on the line of a subsidiary Roman road from St. Albans via Cuffley Ridgeway to Ermine Street. Later it became a junction for coach routes to Newgate Street, Hatfield and Potters Bar.

Agriculture predominated and memory of the Windmill on Cheshunt Common lingers in the name of Millcrest Road. The

GOFF'S OAK 1902

important market gardening which spread up from the Lea Valley in the 19th century has now passed its peak, although there are still some very flourishing nurseries. The railway came to neighbouring Cuffley in 1910 (rather than to Goffs Oak, Lady Meux having refused its encroachment near her estate), and an important function of Goffs Oak now is as a dormitory area for London, although many people commute more locally.

St. James' Church's foundation stone was laid by the High Sheriff of Hertfordshire in 1860, and the Church was consecrated on St. James' Day 25th July 1862 by the Bishop of Rochester, in whose Diocese this area then lay. The cost of building was £2,200, and much of the furnishing at that time came from Cheshunt Church, whose vicar remains Patron to this day. The Rev. John Teague Greenway arrived from Liverpool in 1864 and became vicar when Goffs Oak became a separate parish in 1872. A wall plaque in the chancel cherishes his memory and records that he was vicar until he died in 1919. The Church was built in Rickless Lane, which was then re-named St. James Road. There is still no gas main in the road, and for about 60 years lighting was by means of candles on alternate pews. Electricity was installed in the 1920s, but only now is the heating system of old water pipes being reviewed.

Gosmore 🌺

Gosmore is a small village lying about 1½ miles south of Hitchin off the A600. If the High Street is approached from the north, a letter box will be seen built into a brick wall, hence the name Letter Box Row for the adjoining cottages. In the garden of these cottages is a well which at one time was the water supply for the whole village.

The pond was in the centre of the village in front of the village green. This was used by the drovers from nearby villages to rest and water their cattle when taking them each Tuesday to sell at Hitchin market.

Opposite the green, now known as the Recreation Ground, there was a bakery in the now named Olde Cottage where the old bread oven can still be seen. Local residents would leave their Sunday joint to be roasted while they attended church.

Victoria Farm was originally a dairy farm with fruit orchards but all this land at the rear of the house has been developed for residential purposes.

On the Green, often referred to as the Close, stood a wooden building on bricks used as a Church Army Mission Hall and the surrounding ground within the hedge was consecrated ground. During the week children gathered in the hall for religious talks and games.

At one time Gosmore had its own village hall, a wooden building, also on the Close, where dances and other social gatherings took place.

Turning right at the crossroads into Maidencroft Lane an inn, the Red Cow, was sited on the right opposite Avenue Farm. Further on, in the grounds of Hindmount there was once a chapel used for services on Sunday evenings. To continue, a Water Garden Centre will be passed on the right before the imposing residence of Maidencroft Manor comes into view. It is reputed that Henry VIII used this as a hunting lodge and once, when partaking in one of his favourite sports, fell from his horse into the river Hiz.

Returning to the High Street, on the opposite corner to The Bull stood two cottages with thatched barns. In these, children's parties were held on special occasions. Opposite the old shop stands Holly Tree Cottage, and in the wall can be seen a little window where the local cobbler used to sit mending shoes. There was once a coal and wood merchant in Mill Lane, but this land has all been developed.

Gosmore now shares religious and social facilities with the adjoining village of St. Ippolyts.

Graveley 🦢

According to the old milestone in Graveley's High Street, the village lies 33 miles from London. Most people see only the buildings which stand along either side of this main street, once the busy Great North Road, but more line Church Lane to the east and climb the hill to the west to meet the old parish boundary — the Roman road which connected Baldock with St. Albans.

The village owes its present position to the route of the main road, for the Saxons had settled in a sheltered valley about half a mile to the east, where earthworks can still be seen near Graveley Hall Farm and St. Mary's Church. As the population became more mobile and roads became more important new houses were built and the old village was gradually deserted.

The parish of Graveley also includes the hamlet of Chesfield which was originally a separate parish and also had an ancient church, now, sadly, in ruins.

Many of the houses in Graveley are very old, a few dating back to the 16th century, but they have been modernised over the years – timber frames hidden behind pebbledashing and colour wash or Georgian brick fronts. Agriculture, of course, was always important and in the 17th century there were five farms in the High Street with another three along Church Lane and three in Chesfield.

In 1720 the main road through Graveley was taken over by a Turnpike Trust which was responsible for keeping it in a passable condition. To provide money for this purpose toll gates were set up at various points along the road. There was a gate at the north end of Graveley known as Graveley Pinch and another in Stevenage. Wily travellers discovered, however, that by taking an alternative route through Graveley they could miss the Stevenage toll. Not to be thwarted, the Trustees of the Turnpike set up another gate but then many of the Graveley folk were charged the toll just to work in their fields. The Rector, therefore, made special representation to the Trustees, and the inhabitants obtained free use of the gate. Others were not so lucky and a Weston farmer was so incensed at the toll that he ordered his men to pull the gate down. Eventually the toll became uneconomical but the keeper's house remains in Oak Lane.

One of the most attractive features of Graveley is the pond, originally named Causey Pond because of the causeway (now a private drive) which divides it. For many years this was the main source of water for those who had no well. In the 1880s a communal pump was erected in Oak Lane, tapping a natural spring, and, although not in working order, it still stands on the original spot.

Unfortunately, the village shop has been closed recently, but earlier this century, Graveley was served by its own butcher, baker, general store and Post Office, and other goods were delivered. Bill Hitch collected his fish fresh from Stevenage Station, and his call of 'Cod fish! Fresh herring! Fine Dabs! Fine Dabs!' as he pushed his hand cart, could be heard from one end of the village to the other. After retirement he became the school 'Lollipop Man', being a great favourite with the children.

Perhaps the only time that Graveley ever made headline news was in 1912. During a large scale army exercise a Duperdussin monoplane on observation duties crashed in a field adjoining the George and Dragon public house, never reaching its intended landing place near Willian. The pilot and observer died instantly and full page pictures of the wreckage appeared in the national newspapers as these were the first fliers to be killed on active service. An obelisk was set up on the roadside between Gt. Wymondley and Willian causing some historians to mistake this for the site of the crash.

There was more action during the First World War when a Zeppelin was spotted overhead. One old lady fled from her house in terror to shelter with friends, leaving the door locked and a light shining in the window. Luckily a quick witted neighbour covered the window with his coat and the Zeppelin passed over dropping its bombs harmlessly in open fields to the north of the village.

Graveley is still a closely knit and friendly community with several families going back to the 18th and one to the 16th century. Newcomers are welcomed and made to feel at home, but in the face of the ever-spreading new town of Stevenage, the village hopes to retain its unique identity and independence.

Great Amwell

Amwell, Emmewell in the Domesday Book, 'in the hundred of Hertford, of fourteen and a half hides with land for sixteen ploughs', was well established even then and had been the property of Earl Harold and Edward the Confessor. Later it expanded to include parts of present-day Hertford and Hoddesdon. Now it is a scattered village of 2,800 voters spread over an area between the river Lea, the A10 and the A414. It has two public houses and some light industry along the Lea.

The hub of the village lies eccentrically just south of the Lea Navigation Canal, where the church stands above Amwell Pool on the New River. Here too is Emma's Well from which the name probably comes. In the grounds of Well House but hard by the road, its grassy banks planted with aconites, primroses and daffodils, it is much visited throughout the year.

'Emma' is popularly supposed to relate to Canute's wife but is almost certainly older.

It was in 1609 that Sir Hugh Myddleton started work on the New River to carry the water of Chadwell Spring (then also in

Amwell) the 26 miles to Clerkenwell to provide water for the growing London. Opposite Emma's Well the river widens to a pool and on two small islands are monuments to its architect placed there in 1800 by Robert Mylne, himself engineer and architect, whose family lived here until recently.

The Pool and its islands are beautifully kept by the Thames Water Authority and here every year in June the Haileybury Madrigal Society, singers from the College and local communities, give a concert from the larger island to a throng on the banks. The music, the floodlight on the trees and the water, combine to make a magic few of us care to miss.

The village holds an annual flower show and every second year a Flower Festival when, for the whole Whitsun weekend, we keep 'open house'. Several gardens are open (tea is served in some); there is music in the decorated church; a fete and a craft market. The destruction by fire of the old Vicar's room has limited other exhibitions in the last years but the new Parish Hall will provide for these and other village gatherings in future.

The village has a happy atmosphere, typified by its Flower Festival when we welcome many outsiders. Among them are members of another 'Amwell Society', which flourishes at the London end of the New River where many streets bear the Amwell name.

Hadley

Just 13 miles north of London the traveller unexpectedly reaches a lovely area of grass, trees and ponds, surrounded by the most elegant Georgian houses and a few charming old cottages. This is the southern-most point of the village.

Many famous names are linked with this area. Thackeray's grandfather was buried in the churchyard as was Anthony Trollope's sister. Stanley Livingstone rested here for a few years on his return from Africa in 1857, and a more recent resident was Robert Carr who later took the title of Lord Carr of Hadley.

To the east of the Green past the Wilbraham Almshouses (founded in 1777 for 'six decayed housekeepers') is the beautiful church of Monken Hadley, almost the oldest building in Hadley. The date 1494 can be clearly read above the door on the west tower, but a church or chapel stood on the site long before that as a stone tablet in the church porch shows, listing curates, chaplains, and vicars as far back as John, 1244. The church boasts a fine beacon, 'a rare survival from the past', and put there by the monks to guide wayfarers across Enfield Chace, the name given to the area of Hadley Common and the Woods which stretched beyond into Enfield and Waltham Cross. In later times it became a military asset and was used on Easter Eve 1471 to guide the Earl of Warwick's forces on their way to the Battle of Barnet. In 1587 it signalled the approach of the Spanish Armada. It was lit at the Coronation and Silver Jubilee of King George V, at the Peace Celebrations in 1919, the Quincentenary Celebrations of the Battle of Barnet in 1971, and most recently at Queen Elizabeth II's Silver Jubilee. The church contains many interesting brasses and tablets and its beauty has inspired many artists, not least among them being William Turner who painted it in 1793 when he was 18 years old.

Admiral Byng owned a considerable amount of land around the village and his descendants still live in Wrotham Park, the estate which borders the village to the north. It lies between the Great North Road (A1000) and the old main road to the North now known as Kitts End Road. When Dick Turpin roamed the highways this was quite a thriving village with the many inns catering for the travellers on the stagecoaches – now it is a quiet country lane.

The name Hadley is derived from the Saxon 'head heagh' or high place, it being 400 feet above sea level and the highest point between London and York. 'Highstone' was presumably named after the stone obelisk erected in 1740 to commemorate the Battle of Barnet which was fought here in 1471 between the Lancastrians led by the Earl of Warwick and the Yorkists led by King Edward IV. This was one of the most important battles and one of the last in the 100 years of Civil War – known as the War of the Roses. Many relics from this battle can be seen in the Barnet Museum together with the stocks which were originally in position on the western side of Hadley Green, and last used in 1860 for a gambling offence.

Hadley is an area of great interest, not only because of its history but because so much of it is timeless. It is a Conservation Area and great care is taken with repairs and new buildings, and is well worth a visit.

Hadley Wood 🦒

If you race down from Scotland by train, Hadley Wood is a name you will not quite see as the train flashes through the station set in a cutting between two tunnels.

But this is the last outpost of rural Hertfordshire before London. Within seconds, the passenger finds the lush greenery and woodlands turning into estates of little houses, factories, gasworks, and then the increasing grime of the approaching capital.

Yet only 14 miles from Kings Cross are meadows and streams and the tree-lined avenues which grew like a lush oasis where the Great Northern Railway built its station just 100 years ago. Before that, Hadley Wood was a remnant of the great Enfield Chace, one of the royal hunting forests, with nothing but wood and farmland and scattered cottages.

Londoners of more than middle age will tell you that they used to go out to Hadley Wood for picnics and rambles, when they were children. Would they recognise it now? Probably not; like everywhere else, there have been changes.

Hadley Wood people are no longer country folk. Nobody has a small holding, nobody keeps goats, or even chickens. But the matrons of the parish walk their dogs over the fields, and wear good green wellies and camelhair coats, or turquoise jumpsuits and fake fur jackets. And at home, in their neat and pretty kitchens, they bottle jam and brew wine, microwave the dinner, and ice birthday cakes. Their children are packed into the Volvo to get them safely to school, and spend their summer afternoons racing along the pavements on BMX bikes, or hurrying from ballet class to violin lesson.

It was not always thus: there was a family of rumbustical Booth children, whose father built them a large house five minutes from the station and raised them to the warcry of 'Blood and Fire!'; there were two strange ladies, one of whom wrote *The Well of Loneliness*, and was known as John; there was a gardener who bicycled to work, carrying on his lap a blind poodle. There was a cottage which was used as a convalescent home for shell-shocked soldiers of the Great War, and houses that were taken over by the Admiralty or by London-based business looking for a safe haven during the last war. And there was a refined private school which flourished sixty years ago, of which no trace remains, the grounds now turned into a quiet cul-de-sac of desirable houses.

Hadley Wood is certainly desirable. What driver, speeding along Beech Hill in a mad dash from the M25 to the A1000, would not wish himself master of one of those handsome detached houses, so convenient for the golf course? What town child, trudging up the hill from East Barnet or on the bus from Enfield, with fishing-rod and sandwiches, would not love to spend his summer days by Jack's Lake, or searching for butterflies in the nature reserve of Covert Way? Down by the railway, behind the last row of houses, Hadley Woods are deep and mysterious. But they are peripheral to the doings of Hadley Wood ratepayers; community life takes place at the church or the school gates, at the Golf Club or in one another's homes, where ladies learn lampshade-making or Christmas cookery, where Coffee Mornings are held for M.S., and Bring and Buy sales for the RSPCA. Charitable initials abound, and first names, and local gossip.

Even in commuterland, home-computerland, a village heart beats strongly.

Handside 🍂

Handside is now a part of Welwyn Garden City but the area in which it stands has been settled since prehistoric times. Traces of Neolithic and Belgic settlements have been found and the Roman villa of Lockleys is not far away. A village called Haneshyde is recorded in the 13th century. When Ebenezer Howard created his Garden City in the 1920s there was just a hamlet of 8 houses and a well with no Church, shops or pub. Two farms, Upper and Lower Handside, were connected to the village by a narrow country lane.

The oldest remaining buildings date from the 17th century; a cottage dated 1604 in Bridge Road is still lived in. An old barn which was part of Lower Handside Farm is now well-known in the county as The Barn Theatre. In the past this had associations with John Bunyan who is believed to have preached there. It was originally in the village but was moved to its present site when Lower Handside Farmhouse was built at the time of Waterloo. In the early days of the theatre Flora Robson, then an employee of The Shredded Wheat Company, ran one of several drama groups that later amalgamated to form the Barn Theatre Club. It was the only theatre in Hertfordshire entirely owned and run by amateurs. The Barn is reputed to have its ghost; this has never been seen but members working late at the theatre claim to have sensed a 'presence'.

Some of the first houses in the new town were built in Handside Lane. Even before then a local resident remembered seeing the well-known Hertfordshire personality George Bernard Shaw cycling down the lane. Later he was often seen in the town. There are still people who remember the green fields. We are reminded of these in the present road names, such as Moneycroft (now Mannicotts), High Grave (now High Grove), Long Croft and Dognell Green.

People also remember the horse-drawn water cart that delivered water to the first residents. There are even now a few 'gumbooters' who were the first commuters. There were no made-up roads then, only muddy paths, so they wore gumboots to walk to the railway station and left them there until they returned home at night. Life in a new town was not easy!

As Handside saw the beginning of Welwyn Garden City it contains much of the early history of the town. Many of the newer residents are probably unaware that they live in a one-time hamlet. Today they enjoy the pleasant surroundings and facilities which result from the foresight of the early pioneers in town planning.

Harpenden 🌿

A newcomer to Harpenden could argue, with some justification, that he lives in a town, but those with family roots firmly embedded in local soil still think of the centre as 'The Village'. Of course, time has removed some of the old features, such as the village pond and the smithy. Cottages have been replaced by shops and flats and the dusty street is now a stretch of yellow-lined tarmacadam. So, how does Harpenden manage to preserve its village identity?

It does so by retaining its open spaces – the Common, with its cricket pitch and golf courses and also Rothamsted Park – its mass of trees, amongst which is the uncanny horse chestnut in the Lower High Street which always buds, blossoms and sheds its leaves earlier than other trees, and then, right in the heart of the village is Church Green. It was here in years past that the funfair was held, huntsmen and hounds met, and cattle came to drink from the pond. None of these things happen there now – the sound of hooves has given way to the noise of car engines and the pavements are alive with people scurrying about their daily business. However, travelling showmen still return every Bank Holiday, and in September for the 'Statty Fair' (but to the Common now, near the 'Baa-Lamb Trees'), bringing with them their coconut shies, roundabouts and many updated attractions, all alive with flashing lights and loud music – and the smell of candy floss rises above it all.

Without question it was the railways which led to Harpenden's expansion. In 1860 Manland Common was bisected by a single line of railway which ran from Dunstable to Hatfield. Hissing steam engines and clattering carriages shattered the peace of this area of grazing land – the age of the train had arrived in Harpenden, albeit that the station was well away from the village centre. However, as the railway became accepted, so the village began to grow, and when the Midland Railway Company ploughed through with its iron road, even closer to the village, it was only natural that people would take advantage of the more direct link with London. In consequence, one development followed another, 'desirable residences within easy reach of the station' shot up all around, business contacts were made and contracts signed and sealed – Harpenden prospered through ease of communication. Coal and raw materials came in by rail and trains took away animals, watercress and nursery produce. They brought in thoroughbreds for the race meetings held on the common until 1914, together with an unsavoury bunch of London pickpockets, intent on profiting from the gentry who rallied for this prestigious event.

Sadly, the bustle of goods coming and going is yesterday's railway scene. Goods sheds and sidings disappeared years ago, but Harpenden's remaining station has been preserved and well restored, and the Midland main line itself has undergone considerable alterations to enable electrification to be effected. With new fast train services on the 'Bed-Pan Line' (as it is cruelly nicknamed after Bedford and St. Pancras), it is no wonder our village is becoming more and more a community of commuters.

It is ironic that the branch lines which played so great a part in the working life of the community now offer commuters a chance to relax in the peace of the countryside. The original Great

Northern branch, which suffered Dr. Beeching's axe, is maintained as The Lea Walk, whereas the branch from Harpenden to Hemel Hempstead suffered a slow death since 1947 when passenger services were withdrawn following post-war coal shortages. It too, recently became a footpath and cycleway, with a lone restored signal surviving to remind ramblers of the former 'Nickey Line'.

With so much of Harpenden's heritage attributable to those railways, it is interesting to know that part of that heritage is being preserved at Harpenden's own Railway Museum. You will not find rolling stock, nor miles of track, and unfortunately it is not often open to the public, but in a house in north Harpenden live a couple of enthusiasts devoted to the task of collecting old items of railway memorabilia, particularly those with local interest, ranging from paperwork to platform barrows, seats to signals and lamps to lever frames. Collections of local railway photographs and files of historical research complete the museum.

Summing up Harpenden in a few words is not easy, but it is a 'village growing up'; retaining sufficient charm and character and yet moving with the times to provide homes, shops and leisure facilities for its ever-increasing population.

Hertford Heath 🐾

On a part of Roman Ermine Street, which ran from London to York, on the road taken by kings and queens to Hertford Castle to escape London's plagues, Hertford Heath has always been on the edge of history.

Not even one proper village, but a growing together of two, Hertford Heath and Little Amwell, it just grew ... like Topsy.

Mains water came to the village in 1908 and before this time some households had their own well or shared one with a neighbour and many villagers used the pump on the Village Green. But, in November 1897 the water was found to be 'not safe for a public supply' its appearance being 'turbid, yellow, with much foreign matter and sediment'. So, the Chairman of the Parish Council, the Reverend C. W. Barclay, who was also the parish priest 'decided to have a well sunk in his own grounds at his own expense and if he obtained sufficient water he would present same to the parish. ... This liberal and most generous offer was received by the meeting with such a feeling that no words of the Council could express their thanks or those of the Parish for this magnanimous offer and all felt that everybody concerned could only accept the offer in the kindly spirit it was put to them' (Parish Council Minutes 1897).

By 17th June 1898 the well, sunk at the vicarage to 200 feet, was in use. The wind pump installed by Merryweather and Company helped to fill two large tanks in the vicarage and the overflow was pumped up to a tank on the Green for the villagers.

Also installed was 'a fountain on the green in front of the present water pump' for the use of the children.

At this time the village had a particular need for a plentiful water supply. Many of the women took in washing from Haileybury, Balls Park, Brickendonbury and Christ's Hospital. They all had their own drying greens on the Village Greens. One older resident recalls the drying of Christ's Hospital washing – 'one couldn't see the Green for large voluminous bloomers blowing in the wind'.

It was not until January 1909 that the water supply from the vicarage ceased. The Reverend Barclay wrote in the Parish Magazine: 'The laying of the Metropolitan Water Board's main throughout our village ends all difficulty with respect to the Water Supply either now or in the future. For many weeks I gave anxious consideration to the question whether or no I was right to promote the scheme and close my supply, for unless I undertook to do so the Board refused to lay the main. Taking all things into consideration I felt strongly that the welfare of the village must not in any way be sacrificed by my own feeling of disappointment at no longer having the pleasure of supplying the water. . . .'

Hertingfordbury 🌿

A picturesque village which lies just over one mile west of the County Town of Hertford yet still retaining a truly rural atmosphere. The A414 village by-pass, constructed in 1974, slices diagonally across the river Mimram exposing some remarkable scenic beauty.

The green pastures sloping down to the river on either side have sheep and cattle grazing peacefully regardless of passing traffic.

The northern boundary of the village is flanked by a back-cloth of Beech woods, the fringe of The Panshanger Park. This estate was designed in 1801 for the 5th Earl Cowper by landscape architect Humphrey Repton. More recent owners, the Desborough family, sold up in 1953. The mansion was dismantled and the parkland purchased by a gravel company. Public footpaths, however, cross the Park and vistas of its former glory can still be appreciated. The remaining 'King of the Park', the historic Panshanger Oak is tucked away in what were formerly the Pleasure Gardens of Panshanger. The oak (which has a preservation order on it) must be over 500 years old. 250 years ago it was referred to as the 'Great Oak' and is considered by some historians to be the oldest oak tree in England!

Opposite the farm is the 18th-century Water Mill. It ceased milling in 1933 but corn drying still takes place using the only gas drying plant in the county. An early miller – Thomas Newman – presented to the parish the church clock which today still strikes out the hours. Thomas Newman died in 1870 aged 88 years.

Towards the end of the 19th century the coaching trade was replaced by a newer form of personal transport. A Womens Institute member recalls her Edwardian childhood when 'flocks of bicyclists would arrive to refresh themselves, and on summer Sundays a harpist would play outside the door to entertain them having carried his harp all the way from Hertford and back'.

Between the wars coaches again stopped in front of the White Horse – this time the bustling charabanc trade – but nowadays travellers of a different sort frequent the old inn. It was recently purchased by Trust House Forte who modernised and extended it and during the week it is now the haunt of commercial travellers and other business folk.

Before 'biding awhile' at the White Horse or the other local, The Prince of Wales, take a quiet stroll along St. Mary's Lane until you reach the old bridge which spans the road. There you will discover the Cole Green Way. This is a disused railway track now a popular countryside walk managed by Herts County Council. Scrubland has been allowed to develop on either side which provides ideal habitat for wildlife. It is a happy hunting ground for many types of birds including tits, warblers, finches and blackcaps. Green woodpeckers can often be heard in the nearby woods.

Hexton ✤

Within living memory Hexton village has changed very little in appearance, and old friends returning after a long absence are glad to find it so. The wooded hills and valleys lying to the south, the ivy covered walls, trim houses and gardens along the street and the surrounding farmland give a sense of peace and continuity. Nearly half the working population work in the parish, and are mostly still connected with the land.

Only ten new houses have been added to the forty four which were standing early this century. Two of the ten were built on the site of the last old thatched cottage in which Mrs. Beatrice Chance lived for all her 96 years. She was one of the great characters in the village whose interest in life never waned despite the changes all around her. She, who had seen a lord of the harvest set out with his mowers and scythes, watched huge combines pass her door with the same keen eye.

Present day Hextonians can join in the activities of the 800 year old church, the school, the cricket and football clubs, the W.I., the social club, Village Hall, youth club or playgroup. They can pop into the Post Office, have a drink at the Raven, climb the hills, or stroll the lanes and see the work of the farming year. Many are glad that the traffic along the top road sweeps by the village without a glance.

The present manor house, built about 1770 on the site of an older farm house, superseded the Burystead which lay near the church. It was the home for over 70 years of Caroline Young and her French husband, Joseph de Lautour, whom she, at sixteen, had met and married as a dashing young Ensign in the Guards. His family had been forced to leave France during the Revolution. The couple lived in tremendous style, adding two wings on to the house, laying out the park, pleasure grounds and gardens, and entertaining lavishly. They employed most of the population on the farm and estate and also on building projects for the church, the new village pump and the new school. Caroline was a strong character, a loving mother of eight, a careful manager and a compassionate landlord. After her death in 1869 the fortunes of the village fell to a very low ebb.

Thirty years later a Yorkshire industrialist saw the tumbledown cottages and unkempt farms and determined to make a model estate. George Hodgson spent thousands of pounds restoring and re-building. He laid out the cricket pitch and quoits pitch and even a marbles playing area. He restored the manor house, adding a tower and flag pole, and planted 250,000 conifers on the hills.

Since then Hexton and farming have prospered steadily. During the wars sons were lost and anxiety shared but no bomb fell, and the peace and seclusion appeared unaltered. The old village self sufficiency has given way to the inter-dependence common now to all – the public services of water, electricity, welfare, sewerage etc., have replaced the old customs and craftsmen of earlier days. Unusual events in the last forty years were when the church tower collapsed, two fierce fires broke out, a freak snow storm trapped a hundred people in the village for the night, two friendly female ghosts were seen, lead thieves robbed the church roofing and a swan kept wicket at a Sunday afternoon match.

Traffic has increased and modern farm technology and machinery have changed the face of the land, but much that is now rare elsewhere remains – village friendliness and good neighbourliness, quiet lanes and streams, space and tranquillity.

High Cross

At the top of the hill, coming from Wadesmill, on the left is the estate of Marshalls. There was a Saxon settlement on the site, but the present house dates back only to 1906. The property was in the Martin-Leake family for over two hundred years. Colonel Arthur Martin-Leake, an Army Surgeon, won the Victoria Cross twice. The first time in South Africa and then in World War One. Opposite is Marshalls Farm, one of the only two remaining dairy farms within the village boundary. Working on the farm for Mr. Pateman is Mr. Cliff Carrick, who as well as being an authority on horses, was the last horse bargeman to work on the river Lea in Ware.

The Parish Church, St. Johns, is only one hundred and twenty years old. It has some fine Victorian stained-glass windows. The nearby Giles-Puller School was opened in 1866. Just to the north of the school is Sutes Farm, with its early 17th-century moated farmhouse, the moat being fed by a spring and land drains. The farm was part of the Youngsbury Estate but was sold in 1956.

Opposite Sutes Farm is Pest House Lane, where the hospital for plague victims once stood. The patients were brought out from

ON THE SPOT
WHERE STANDS THIS
MONUMENT
IN THE MONTH OF JUNE
1785
THOMAS CLARKSON
RESOLVED
TO DEVOTE HIS LIFE
TO BRINGING ABOUT
THE ABOLITION
OF THE
SLAVE TRADE

London by river to Ware. There is nothing at all of the hospital still there. The lane ends at Standon Green End, opposite Standon Green End Farm where there is another 17th century farm house with parts of the house dating back to 1550. This is the other dairy farm.

Also in a field in Standon Green End there is a monument to mark the spot where Vincenti Lunardi, the first aeronaut over British soil landed in his hot air balloon on 15th September 1784. He had taken off from Bunhill Row, Finsbury in London and travelled over Barnet, St. Albans, Codicote, Welwyn, Tewin and Bengeo before landing.

High Wych

Instead of turning off through Harlow on the re-routed A414, it is pleasant to travel through some of Hertfordshire's prettiest villages. On each side of the High Wych Road, there are wide stretches of open farmland with beautiful old houses nestling in small coppices within their grounds. First, one reaches Pye Corner with its line of houses and its ancient public house, now disfigured by protective steel barriers, but beware of the bend! Speedy motorists have been known to crash into the pub's old oak dining room.

Continuing safely along this road, one reaches the village of High Wych. The 'y' of 'Wych', is pronounced to rhyme with the 'i' of High, much to the discomfort of those W.I. members who try to write limericks beginning

'there was an old man of High Wych'

Here, the new primary school hides behind the flintstone old school whose hall provides a useful meeting-place for church and school. Next to the old school is the flintstone church of St. James the Great, aptly named for it is the exact replica of a fishermen's church in Great Yarmouth as St. James is the patron saint of fishermen.

The interior of the church is decorated with a design of red vine leaves and contains the text of the Beatitudes on the arch of the chancel, now sadly showing that they have been there for over 100 years. The first vicar of this church was the priest who later became Bishop Johnson, the first to live at the old vicarage opposite the church, now called The Grange.

The Grange is now a gentleman's residence. It is built in the same style and material as the church and is surrounded by sweeping farmland. The old glebe cottages are near there as well and another old house formerly called Wychcroft is believed to be haunted.

Adjacent to the church is the Village Memorial Hall, beautifully refurbished by a local architect so that now it is one of the best in the district. On the far side of this, the road bends to the left past thatched cottages which are floodlit at night. These belong to the local builder who maintains them as offices. Several times, these have helped to bring an award to High Wych as one of the Best-Kept Villages.

The road passes between the village playing fields and the village stores, past the Manor of Groves, once the home of the Buxtons, and several modern and ancient cottages before striking across the fields to Allen's Green. Though several miles from High Wych, Allen's Green is part of the same parish, sharing the same school, though it once had one of its own. It has its own tiny flintstone church of great beauty and the village people open their hearts to all who worship there. Now alas, its one-time peace is shattered every morning and evening when cars rush through, carrying their impatient occupants to places beyond this little village, which has no post office, no shop, no library of its own though it has a good hall and a good public house.

Allen's Green is well worth a visit but its inhabitants would much rather see you on foot, visiting the haunted houses, the underground passages, the old wartime airfield and the part of the sweeping countryside where a notorious criminal lived in a tent, undiscovered for several months.

Hinxworth ✺

Hinxworth is not a well known village; our claim to fame is that we are the most northerly village in Hertfordshire. A collection of houses, situated 1½ miles from the A1, a Church, The Three Horseshoes Public House, and a Village Hall, but the folk here are a close caring community, where the joys and sorrows of all are shared.

The village church of St. Nicholas, 800 years old, stands smiling and serene at the end of an avenue of ten lime trees. These trees were planted many years ago, to represent the Clutterbuck family, mother, father, and eight children, and they are now a memorial to them.

There are not many of the old families left now, two great wars and the passage of time has dwindled the numbers, to be replaced by the 'young ones', but the village still thrives by the 'new' folk moving in.

Very few people actually work in the village itself, but commute to the nearest towns, but thankfully the village atmosphere has not been lost. It has changed, of course, but we still have our community closeness and spirit which to us spells Hinxworth.

The Hormeads 🦢

Listed in the Domesday Book as three separate Manors, Great and Little Hormead and Hare Street are now known as one parish – The Hormeads. Hare Street lies on the main road from Puckeridge. Little Hormead is about half a mile off the main road and Great Hormead is further on. They are situated in such a way that they roughly form a triangle.

The Hormeads have a long history. Changes have taken place, but their beauty and charm lies in the fact that a number of the houses still in existence were either already standing in the year 1500 or were built within the following century. There are about 280 houses in all three villages. Today they are a mixture of styles due to renovations and extensions. With the exception of outlying farmhouses, the houses were built alongside the main road. In most cases the church was built next to the Manor house, so that the respective lord of the manor could walk to church across his front garden.

St. Nicholas church is similarly situated. There has been a church on this site since Saxon times. The original was of stone but today only the font remains from this period. Over the years alterations, renovations and additions have been made. In 1872 the whole church was restored. Since then restoration work has continued.

While Great and Little Hormead have been united for some 160 years, Wydiall was added a few years ago. The three parishes are now with one incumbent, and one P.C.C. Each church building retains its traditional church wardens who are responsible for the care of the churches. The majority of the church services are held in St. Nicholas, while St. Mary's at Little Hormead, which has no heating or lighting, is used only infrequently. The people of the three parishes, however, are now interchanging and moving freely between the three churches.

There is a team of bellringers who ring on Sundays and festivals. Tuesday night is practice night. The bells were re-cast soon after the Second World War. The handbells are also used on special occasions.

The Hormead mills were once a feature of the village, but have long since gone.

The river Hor runs down to the river Quin at Hare Street, alongside the bottom road. It is little more than a drainage ditch but after a heavy rainfall the water floods the road in places.

Little Hormead has some thirty-seven houses and a Norman church. It has been kept in good repair and attracts many visitors.

Although Hare Street is a hamlet Hare Street House is used as a residence for the catholic community and has a small chapel in its grounds. Past Cardinals have used the house as a summer residence.

Today the Hormeads lay claim to two pubs, the Beehive at Hare Street and the Three Tuns at Great Hormead.

The village retains its friendly community spirit although today it is regarded more as a commuter area rather than a place where people work as well as reside.

Hunsdon 🦐

Hunsdon is mentioned in the Domesday Book. In 1086 it had 360 acres under the plough, also a mill and a resident priest, which was unusual in those days. It is almost certain that there was a wooden church where the present building now stands, a mile from the centre of the village. The present building was dedicated to Saint Dunstan in the 19th century, but a will of 1392 bequeaths a vestment and chalice to the Church of Blessed Mary of Hunsdon, and a later will contains a request to be buried in the churchyard of Our Lady of Hunsdon but in still later wills it is simply the Parish Church. Early in the 15th century a church was built by Sir John Tyrell and the chapels were added in the 16th and 17th centuries.

Close by the Church stands Hunsdon House, a much favoured residence of Henry VIII. Sir Henry Chauncey wrote: 'The King made choice of this seat for the Breeding and Education of his Children in respect of the Air.' The royal children including Elizabeth I stayed in Hunsdon House and worshipped in the church. Henry came to escape the Plague, he loved to hunt and had an extensive Deer Park. 'Hunsdon House' a stately country dance is attributed to Henry VIII and was probably performed when he was entertaining in Hunsdon. The first house was built by Sir William Oldhall in 1454 and was rebuilt by Henry VIII in 1525. It was acquired by Elizabeth I in 1558 and she gave it to her cousin John Carey who she created Lord Hunsdon. Over the years it had many different owners but in the late 18th century it came into the hands of an influential family, the Calverts, who owned Bonningtons and Nine Ashes. It was rebuilt by Nicholson Calvert who was a member of Parliament. So a Tudor Palace became a substantial Georgian mansion in the early 19th century.

The Hunsdon Park of Henry's time was extensive and probably included the Gatehouse and White Horses and other old properties in the centre of the village, some of which are of the 16th century. The Pump House is one of the oldest properties. The first documentary evidence of what then must have been an old house is dated 1637. It has been at different times an inn, a coach-builders and wheelwrights, and an antique shop. Both sides of the High Street have old cottages which are well maintained in black and white giving a pleasing centre to the village. Another interesting property about the same age as The Pump House is Old House in Widford Road which in 1690 was an inn known as The Wheatsheaf.

Behind the Pump House is Drury Lane leading to the land which was developed as an aerodrome in World War II. The Turkey Cock Inn and several cottages had to be demolished in Acorn Street to make room for the runway.

Hunsdon Lodge Farm, demolished in 1946, was probably 16th century but there remains a wooden barn, still in use, which is thought to have been part of the Hunting Lodge used by Henry VIII. The Turkey Cock moved to temporary premises in Widford Road and there are two other public houses in the centre near the pump, The Crown and The Fox and Hounds.

The Village Hall lies in the centre of the village. It was used as a school for many years until the present school was erected in

1926. It has since been extended and now caters for about one hundred children up to the age of eleven. There are log books of the school dating from 1868.

Hunsdon is very proud of its timbered Village Hall. It is a meeting place for the villagers. Each Saturday morning coffee is served and friends meet for a chat. The hall is in constant use by the various clubs and associations which cater for people of all ages, from Toddlers Group to the Over Three Score Club. For the more active there is a Tennis Club and a playing field where Summer Fêtes are held.

Hunton Bridge

Today the village of Hunton Bridge is busy with traffic passing through it to reach Abbots Langley and the Rolls Royce factory at Leavesden.

In 1673 it was described as being 'by the highway between Watford and Hemel Hempstead'. To reach the village then it was necessary to travel on narrow rutted roads along Gypsy Lane and Upper Highway which in those days were part of the old Stage Coach route, being on higher ground.

An early grave in Langleybury churchyard is that of Ruddy Faulkner a one-time coach driver on the London to Brighton run, and has a milestone on his grave. With the building of the railways in the mid 19th century stage coaches became obsolete. Now Gypsy Lane is closed to traffic and the A41 is a dual carriage road which by-passes the village.

In Upper Highway there are still several Elizabethan cottages, and the Unicorn Inn still supplies refreshments to thirsty travellers. The old inn sign used to depict a Unicorn on each side with the words 'I believe in you' on one side and 'If you believe in me' on the other. A highwayman was hanged opposite the inn and, according to custom, was buried at the nearest crossroads; in this case where Upper Highway crossed Hunter Lane and Hunton Bridge Hill. In 1930 the coffin was found and reburied near the churchyard.

Malt was brewed in the village for hundreds of years. The maltster's cottage was next to the stream crossing the village by culvert. Next door was the Maltsters Arms public house. Malt is still being brewed two miles up the Gade Valley at the Wander factory.

HUNTON BRIDGE WHARF.
C. Andrews 1984

About the year 1800 the Grand Junction Canal was dug and the river Gade supplied much of the water. A low-lying lake west of the hamlet was also drained into it. Horses or mules were used to haul barges to and from London, and six stables were provided at the Kings Head Public House for the animals. A coal wharf was established on one of the two quays.

Because the canal had drained the valley the main road from London to the Midlands was straightened from Gypsy Lane through Kings Langley and Apsley to Boxmoor. In 1858 Mr. William Loyd, who lived at Langleybury paid for a school to be built between the main road and the canal near the bridge. Six years later he had the church built where the lake had been drained. About the same time a chapel was built near the Kings Head. The school remained in use for over one hundred years, until it had to be replaced on a new site because of the increase in the number of children. The old school is now used as offices and the chapel is a glass studio.

Ickleford 🦢

Thought to be merely waste ground at the time of the Domesday Book, Ickleford's site on the Icknield Way, near a crossing in the river (hence the name 'Icknield's–Ford') proved very important.

By the 12th century the new settlement had a church, St. Katharine's, thought in the time of James II to be a fit resting place for a local gypsy king, Henry Boswell. Living to the grand age of ninety, Boswell had travelled the country all his life but chose to be buried near his birthplace alongside his beloved Icknield Way. His grave can still be found in the churchyard.

Nestling on the south side of St. Katharine's is The George, a 15th-century inn which has catered for many a weary wayfarer passing through the village. One such traveller was thought to have been Dick Turpin.

Village life grew to encompass all the usual industries associated with an agricultural community. There were blacksmiths, harness-makers and the notable craft of straw plaiting. The area was famous for providing the material for straw hats, before and around the turn of this century.

There have always been water mills serving the community, some grinding corn and wheat, others barley. This industry exists today in the shape of Bowman Flour Mill which has the most modern premises in England and is one of the biggest independent milling companies. Rural activity was aided by the proximity of Hitchin, a local market town where livestock and produce found buyers.

Around 1900, Walter and Arthur Witter came to Ickleford to found their Ickleford Art Industries, a teaching school for fine arts. The crafts plied by the young ladies and men of the village included fine metalwork, tapestries and needlework. Indeed, the work was of such excellent quality that it attracted patronage from several members of the royal family. Thus the workships were kept busy for forty years.

Back in the time of the Land Enclosure Act in 1776, it was solely thanks to the vigilance of the Lord of the Manor that Common Land Grazing Rights were preserved. Even now all the old houses, public houses and farms in Ickleford possess the right to graze two female cattle on the common.

Benevolent guidance was the order of the day under Squire Fellows who lived at Ickleford Manor in Edwardian times.

The stories are handed down from the memory of Mrs. Emily Newman who was in service at the manor. She remembers a man whose compassion for the poorer villager was enlightened even by modern standards. The village workhouse, Bleak Hall, had been closed by that time and Fellows took it upon himself to see that daily a cooked dinner and one pint of milk was provided for each newly delivered and nursing mother. This continued for a fortnight or until the bodily strength of each woman was regained.

At Christmas each elderly villager received a joint of beef and 1 cwt of coal on which to cook it. The children of estate workers were not forgotten; they went up to the manor to receive a small present, usually a toy.

Villagers' own generosity spilled out to encompass wider issues during the war years. The Great War saw the furnishing of the Old Thatched Cottage for the exclusive use of a family fleeing from Belgium. They were supported throughout the conflict and ties with them were still maintained, even after repatriation.

After the war, smallholdings were developed in the village as a response to Lloyd George's plea to help the returning soldier.

The Second World War saw the formation of an organisation to support the soldier at the front. Apart from clothes packages, the village collected over £1,000 to distribute to the 'lads' when they came home.

During the conflict life had its lighter moments. The story goes that A.R.P. wardens on duty one night found some spent incendiary shells and decided to have some fun with a fellow villager. They gathered up their finds and deposited them neatly outside his cottage. Next morning the gentleman in question was thrilled to think that he had had such a narrow escape from the previous night's raid.

It was during the last war that Mr and Mrs Randolph Churchill lived at the Old Rectory. Mrs. Churchill helped to organise the meals for the evacuees and Winston Churchill visited his son for the christening of a grandchild. A famous visitor at the Rectory was Evelyn Waugh, fresh from his success with *Brideshead Revisited*. He records in his diary that he celebrated V.J. Day in Ickleford and remained drunk all day!

Ickleford continues its traditional principles of application and sensibility into the present day. From dismal and depressing beginnings in 1966 it rose to the challenge and became the Best Kept Village in Hertfordshire in 1983 and 1985.

Kelshall

Look on the map and you will see that the village of Kelshall lies about 550 feet up on the East Anglian Heights, a line of modestly high hills forming the beginnings of the Chilterns.

A walk around Kelshall reveals that although small in size the village is well cared for (winning the Best Kept Hamlet in Hertfordshire in 1984 and being runner-up several times). From a vantage point one gets a delightful panoramic view of immaculately tended fields, reaching into Bedfordshire and Cambridgeshire, green, then golden, as the year progresses, dissected by the railway line to Cambridge and the Icknield Way (today's A505). Beauty surrounds us throughout the year but somehow winter is rather special; we get heavy falls of snow and most years have to wait for the farms to dig the roads clear before we can venture far. One year three cars were completely buried between us and Therfield, a distance of only two miles. The feeling of togetherness amongst our community comes into its own during these wintry days, villagers are ever ready to help dig paths clear, check on housebound elderly neighbours and generally lend a hand whenever needed. Quite a few women regularly drive for Meals-on-Wheels and, even during really bad weather they have never missed a day.

The village responds to every cause with great gusto so it is not surprising that events organised to support the church or Village Hall are the highlights of the year, with everyone participating in some way. The church is unique with every roof-beam decorated with a delicately beautiful floral design together with painted screens of great rarity, so we jealously guard this building, of which we are very proud. The Village Hall was built in 1893 and was the school until 1923; now it serves as Polling-station, venue for parties, dances, Keep-Fit, slide shows and every communal activity typifying village life.

Kelshall is not large enough to have an elected Parish Council, instead we have a well-attended half-yearly Parish Meeting with a Chairman, Treasurer and Secretary.

This is a truly rural farming community but the hobbies and pastimes of some of our residents add extra interest; the arts are represented by a highly gifted lady who does beautiful stained-glass work, a farmer's wife (an acknowledged expert on local history and skilled needlewoman) finds time to illustrate her historical books and articles, another lady restores pine furniture; one man who has lived in the village for many years lovingly recreates an endless variety of spinning-wheels, and a recent arrival is an artist.

This delightful village abounds with loving, caring and talented people, their skills enhance our lives and we are grateful. Those of us who chose to live here consider ourselves most fortunate.

Kimpton 🦡

A local newspaper once dubbed Kimpton a 'sleepy little village', and perhaps passing through one could be forgiven for believing this to be true. However once away from the impassive High Street there is a tremendous amount of activity.

The first weekend in May is one of the main events on the Kimpton Calendar, when the May Festival takes place. This involves the whole community and was started over 21 years ago to raise funds for the Parish Church fabric fund. All the Maytime traditions are upheld. The May Queen, chosen from the Village maidens of about 12 years old, leads a procession through the village and is then crowned on the Green. Each organisation in the village runs a stall or sideshow from which it keeps half of the profit. Various forms of rustic entertainment take place on the Green; the bell tower of the Church is open to the public; and there is usually a craft market, an art display or floral arrangements in the Church. A recent event has been a 'Fun-Run' on the Sunday after May Day, and another very popular attraction is the 'Brains of Kimpton' general knowledge quiz. The finals of this competition are always well attended by supporters of the winning teams.

July is a double anniversary for Kimpton Memorial Hall. On 4th July 1981 the hall was almost completely destroyed by fire in the small hours of the morning. When the community had recovered from the shock it was quick to look to the future and plans were made for rebuilding. The hall is such a focal point for social and sporting life in the village that it was very difficult to be without a meeting place. Every organisation and club held fund raising activities, and with grants and loans from local and regional councils, and some generous individual donations, by

1983 Kimpton had a brand new, bigger and better Memorial Hall. Almost two years from the day of destruction, on 10th July 1983 Kimpton was proud and delighted to welcome Her Majesty Queen Elizabeth the Queen Mother to formally open the new Memorial Hall.

It may not be a picturesque village, although there are several pretty cottages surrounding the Church and Village Green, but there is a tremendous community spirit and over 2,000 residents are happy to call it home.

Kings Langley 🪶

How do we tell the story of our village in one short article? We need a Time Machine to telescope the years into a few minutes. Why not join us on a journey, commencing two thousand years ago.

We begin in a thickly-wooded valley, through which a river flows. All we can see is a few wild animals and, occasionally, hunters seeking food. As the picture changes, from nearby Verulamium (St. Albans) the Romans come. They are building a road on the east side of the river and a small villa too.

As we speed through time, once more the land reverts to wild woodland, the villa becomes a delapidated ruin. We have completed half our journey before there is much change. Now a group of people decide to settle here. They clear a narrow band of land by the river, build some huts and cultivate a few crops.

It is 1066 when we see that something unusual is happening. From the north, along the road from Berkhamsted Castle, comes the army of William the Conqueror. The Saxons have submitted, so William rides in triumph to his Coronation in London, past this Saxon village named 'Langelei' – the long clearing. Within a few years more land has been cleared and there are two water-mills. On the hill which leads up from the west bank of the river a church is being built, near the Manor House of the Norman Chenduit family. They call their Manor Chenduit Langley.

We approach the 14th century and the village becomes the centre of great activity. A large Hunting Park, stocked with deer, is made at the southern end of the village. King Edward I has given the Manor to his wife, Eleanor, and a large palace is being built on the hill above the church and village. Wagons bring in stone, trees are felled for timber and soon the royal family spend much of their time in their new home in what is now called Langley Regina – Queen's Langley.

Continuing on our journey, during the 14th century the palace remains a frequent venue for the monarchs and their families. It is now named Langley Regis (King's Langley). Edward II founds a large Friary beside the palace and orders a sumptuous funeral there for his murdered favourite Piers Gaveston. Great celebrations in 1341 greet the birth here of Edward III's son Edmund of Langley, future Duke of York, Regent of England and ancestor of the Kings of the House of York. Under Royal patronage the village has grown. Many villagers have suffered during the Black Death and there is rioting near the Saracen's Head Inn at the time of the Peasant's Revolt in 1381. Village life now revolves around the Palace, the Mills, the farms and a weekly Thursday Market. In the Newchepinge (New-market), near the recently enlarged Parish Church a Great Fair is held in Whit week; the medieval community is thriving.

Onward towards Elizabethan times we travel. How things are changing! Tudor monarchs are spending less time here, the Palace shows signs of decay. With the Dissolution of the Monasteries, the Friary is in ruins and on Queen Elizabeth's order the tomb of Edmund of Langley is moved, for safety, down the hill to the Parish Church. Without the royal visits, Kings Langley becomes a mainly agricultural community. More land is cleared to make large farms and there are many newly-built half-timbered houses.

Our Time Machine takes us through a time of little change until, in 1792, there is a great upheaval. The valley is invaded by workmen from all areas of the British Isles. Canal builders have arrived to work by the river Gade. Kings Langley is about to feel the impact of the Industrial Age. The Grand Junction (now Grand Union) Canal links us to a country-wide network. Ease of transport encourages the paper-making industry to take over mills in the vicinity and John Dickinson builds Nash and Home Park Mills beside the canal with their own 'modern' workers' cottages.

Just forty years later the navvies are back. This time they work on the eastern side of the valley. The railway has arrived. The main line between London and the Midlands not only carries goods, but encourages a commuter population.

So we travel through the last 150 years, seeing the constant growth of population and the introduction of many innovations.

In the early 19th century a daily School of Industry is founded, later to become the National School. A Cricket Club is formed. In the second half of the century an Association for Mutual Improvement provides a Library and Reading Room. Gas lighting arrives in 1863 and a Drainage and Sewage Scheme thirteen years later. In 1895, a water supply is laid on.

Approaching the 20th century, the High Street is busy with hay and straw carts on their way to the London markets. These, and large timber wagons are joined by troop movements during the 1914–18 War. After the Armistice, in 1919 the Women's Institute is founded; in 1923, the Kings Langley Players and two years later a Bowls Club. The Second World War sees the arrival of many evacuees from London and some German bombs fall on the village and demolish an inn by the canal.

Now we arrive at the present. South of the village we see the newly-built M25 slashing its way across the valley. The High Street, the A41, has a constant flow of traffic but, if you look closely, you can see many echoes of the past. The Common, large open fields and the remains of the Friary, now a private residence are still at the top of the hill. The beautiful Parish Church, with the tomb of Edmund of Langley, stands near the High Street. Our High Street with its 16th and 17th century inns and cottages and imposing 18th and 19th century houses. As in medieval times, in the High Street (Newchepinge) every Thursday morning, local produce is on sale – at the W.I. Market. *Some* things do not change!

Kinsbourne Green ❧

Kinsbourne Green lies between Harpenden and Luton just west of the Hertfordshire/Bedfordshire border. The name derives from the spacious wedge-shaped Kinsbourne Common which dominates the small hamlet. It is flanked on one side by gracious houses and on the other by the main A1080 road. Between the road and the common are a few older cottages, the core of the original settlement.

Until about forty years ago, Kinsbourne Green was a fairly self-contained community. There were, and still are, two churches; St. Mary's which was a dual purpose building used as a school on weekdays; and the Methodist Chapel. Most shopping could be

THE FOX INN, KINSBOURNE GREEN, HERTS.

done at the small parade of shops and refreshment and recreation could be found at the two public houses, one on either side of the main road. The local garage provided well-used public tennis courts and there was plenty of open space on the common for horse riding and other recreations. The Hertfordshire Hunt Kennels were here until the Second World War. The Kennels were built in 1866 in the record time of four months and were said to be the finest in Europe when completed. Mr. Gerard Leigh, of Luton Hoo, the Master of Hounds persuaded three hundred railway navvies to work for him by paying them fourpence a day more than the railway wage, and providing free beer. The grooms and whippers-in lived in the small cottages flanking the Common. No doubt it was the patronage of the Hunt retainers that influenced the choice of The Fox as the name for the nearby public house. Farms surrounded the area, including a poultry farm and extensive glasshouses behind the shops. One of the older farms still has a donkey wheel dating from the 17th century. The farm is on high ground at the top of Kinsbourne Common and the well is 145 feet deep sunk into the chalk. The bucket holds about 18 gallons of water and it took a donkey between 10 and 15 minutes to raise a full bucket. A mechanical pump replaced the donkey at the end of the century but the wheel is still in working order despite not being used for many years.

Increasing demand for houses since the war has seen many of the farms vanish and extensive estates have been, and still are being developed on their sites. The increased population has inevitably altered the small cosy community of the pre-war years but Kinsbourne Green is still regarded with affection by those who live there.

The tennis courts are no more, but the shops remain including a Post Office, a well-stocked general store and a hairdressers. The public houses, The Fox and The Harrow continue to serve as meeting places for the local community and both are popular as eating places in the evenings for many Harpenden families. Also attracting people to the area is a flourishing apple farm which sells several varieties of locally grown English apples and pears. The school closed in 1955 but two new ones were built less than ½ mile away to cater for the increasing numbers of infant and junior aged children now living on the new estates. One of Harpenden's three comprehensive schools was built in 1956 not more than a mile from Kinsbourne Common, so many local children receive their complete education from 5–18 years within easy walking distance of home.

It cannot be said that Kinsbourne Green is a separate village now, but there is still a strong sense of community, and it remains a pleasant and friendly place to live.

Knebworth

Originally Knebworth was a small manor house built like a fortress and surrounded by hundreds of acres of land. It was given to a knight called Eudo Dapifer who was a steward to William the Conqueror, as recorded in the Domesday Book. Then, the house was called 'Chenepeworde', meaning 'the house on the hill'.

During the next four hundred years the house changed hands several times, until in 1492 the first Lytton came to Knebworth and it has been the home of the Lytton family for almost five hundred years, providing work and homes for generations of Knebworth inhabitants.

Sir Robert Lytton was the first to come. Known as Sir Robert of the Peak, he came down from Derbyshire, acquired the Manor House, which he pulled down and started to build an enormous mansion of red Tudor brick. The four sides were built around a central courtyard complete with a gate-house, and this is how it remained until the beginning of the nineteenth century, when, due to neglect over a number of years three sides were demolished, and stucco was added to the remaining wing. By the middle of the century, Sir Edward Bulwer Lytton, the famous novelist, was responsible for adding the copper domes, gargoyles and further castellations so popular at this period.

Knebworth has many claims to fame. Queen Elizabeth I visited, Charles Dickens wrote, and Winston Churchill painted at Knebworth House. The first Viceroy of India, Robert, first Earl of Lytton and his son, Victor (Acting Viceroy and Governor of Bengal), lived here, and his son-in-law, Sir Edwin Lutyens, altered the house and redesigned the gardens. Coming up to date, some very famous pop groups such as the Rolling Stones, Lead Zeppelin and Pink Floyd have performed here.

Without the big house there would have been no village, conveniently situated thirty miles (and then one day's ride) from London. Very little has changed since that time. The villagers still worship in St. Mary's 12th-century church, which stands in Knebworth Park. The one remaining inn is appropriately named The Lytton Arms. The old forge, the village school (closed in the 1960s but now housing nursery school children) one shop and several cottages still exist in this corner of old Hertfordshire.

Lemsford 🌿

Lemsford is 21 miles north from London where the Great North Road crosses the river Lea. Here the valley is bounded by steep slopes at Stanborough. Across the valley the land rises with the church on the skyline. Only yards away from the roaring traffic on the A1(M) the village has quiet charm.

In the valley is an area of watercress beds and springs, now a Nature Reserve, enclosed by a wire fence. With a key to enter, the birdwatcher sees an area of reeds and osiers and pools, which are the haunt of kingfishers.

Lemsford is noted for its Water Mill. This has not ground corn for a long time, but has been used by an engineering firm and is now renovated as offices. A beautiful building to look at, it is the 'Old Mill by the Stream' in the Nelly Dean song, sung by soldiers of the Boer War who were billeted in the village. At the Mill foam pollution on the river was once hedge high until manufacturers altered the ingredients in detergents.

In the 18th century, the village was called Lemsford Mill. In 1726, the Turnpike Trust gravelled and widened the Great North Road from the Toll House at Oldings Corner. From the Bull the road went past the site of the church to turn down the hill, over the bridge and up Brickwall Hill to the Toll House at Ayot Green. Many inns lined the route. The most intriguing name is the Long and Short Arm. On the authority of a W.I. member who was born there in 1900, there was a sign over the road depicting the long arm of a carter and the short arm of the publican with a tankard. The old inn was demolished in 1930, the present building has just been renovated. The old road can still be seen alongside the estate wall, but it is a dead end. Another distinctive inn is the Crooked Chimney.

The Estate at Lemsford is Brocket Hall, given its name in Tudor times by Sir John Brocket. In 1746 the estate was bought by Sir Mathew Lamb of Melbourne, Derbyshire who demolished the old house and commissioned the present pleasant brick mansion. The grounds were landscaped, the river dammed to make a lake and a bridge and waterfall constructed. Peniston Lamb M.P., 1st Viscount Melbourne held wild parties at Brocket Hall. The Prince Regent came and a racecourse was made for him. The 2nd Viscount's wife, Caroline, was mentally unstable and romantically infatuated with Byron. She had to be kept unaware when Byron's funeral cortege passed through the village. Lord Melbourne was Prime Minister in the early days of Queen Victoria's reign. The next occupant was Lord Palmerston, also Prime Minister. The Hall was inherited by Earl Cowper of Panshangar. His family built the Church of St. John the Evangelist in 1859, in the Early English style, sited on the hill by the Entrance Gates to Brocket Hall where the road leads down to the village. The parish was taken out of the very large parish of Bishop's Hatfield.

The end of World War I signalled great changes in this part of Hertfordshire. In 1922, Brocket Hall was sold, and when the new owner became a Baron, he took the title Lord Brocket from the

Estate. In 1919 the Panshangar Estate was for sale. Land was bought by Ebenezer Howard for his planned Welwyn Garden City. Speculative builders erected houses as ribbon development along the main roads. All this brought new residents to the area.

There are footpaths across Brocket Park but the mansion is not open to the public. To walk across the bridge and see the row of picturesque cottages, the 18th century Bridge House, the Sun Inn, by the sparkling river to the Old Mill and Mill House, to climb up the hill to the church and there to breathe the fresh invigorating air from the arable fields and woods is to realise how precious is the Green Belt.

Letchworth 🖋

Letchworth was built on a nucleus of three small villages, Norton to the north, Willian and Letchworth to the south. One of the most important reasons for choosing this site was the fact that there was a source of pure water nearby in the Weston Hills. Ebenezer Howard, who was the founder of the garden city was a Quaker and an idealist. He wanted to provide good housing for people of all financial situations in life, with a decent garden for each house, good working conditions, and no alcohol! The first factories were housed in pre-fabricated buildings, which soon gave way to quite imposing factories, which were constructed on the leeward side of the town, so that any smoke was carried away by the prevailing winds. The most imposing of these factories must surely be the old Spirella building, whose picture travelled countrywide on the corsetry boxes. Though foundation garments are still constructed in the old building, a large percentage of the factory is now given over to a multiplicity of little businesses.

In the early days of the Garden City a competition was held for domestic architecture. Nevell's Road was called Exhibition Road, because this is where a lot of the houses for the competition were built, none to cost more than one hundred pounds at that time. The varying styles of housing in Nevell's Road is reflected in the rest of the towns residential areas, also the tradition of tree-lining the streets. The first inhabitants of the Garden City shopped in one street, Leys Avenue, in little open fronted shops. This has grown into a compact but comprehensive shopping area complete with a nice warm market and modern shopping precinct.

Norton Common, within walking distance of the town centre, is an important sixty acre area of conservation, where muntjac deer and squirrels roam. It is an ideal and beautiful place to walk the dog. On the edge of the common is a well-attended open air swimming pool. This was augmented in 1980 by a modern leisure centre, built at the other end of the town, where swimming can go on summer and winter alike, as well as a lot of other sport and leisure activities.

Many people were drawn to live in Letchworth over a long period because for sixty years it was a temperance town, and there aren't many public houses even today. The Skittles Inn was a temperance house where refreshing teetotal drinks could be enjoyed in good company. Nowadays re-named the Settlement it is open for mind refreshment as people take advantage of the many interesting courses available there.

One does wonder what the old Iron Age men in their fort on the Icknield Way would think of today's town. They would appreciate all the excellent schools, the caring day hospital, the cottage hospital which caters for the elderly who need a stay in hospital and also has an excellent physiotherapy department. The youth centre, the varying churches both ancient and modern, and most of all the thousands of people who make our community what it is, colourful, caring and forward looking.

Leverstock Green ✆

Although Leverstock Green is on the outskirts of Hemel Hempstead and close to the M1 motorway, it still retains a very strong village atmosphere. People passing through would probably note the large village green with its war memorial, the double bell-cot on the west end of the church and the fine topiary animals carefully tended by the owner of Rose Cottage.

Most houses in the village have been built in the last 100 years but there are some interesting old cottages and farmhouses in existence. The Leather Bottle is the oldest public house and stands picturesquely facing the green with its cricket pitch and alongside the small row of modern shops.

In 1551 the village was known as Levelystock Green and we know that 'stock' or 'stocc' meant a tree stump. The Middle Ages saw most of the local land under arable cultivation. Cattle were

106

grazed on the fallows and stubble but at other times when the fields were under crops other grazing was needed. Many lanes had wide verges or 'greens' which were used as pasture at such times. Some of these are still obvious as broad grass verges, but others are partially overgrown so that the lane appears to be bounded by copses. High Street Green and Green Lane are two examples of this in the village.

In the 17th century the village had a thriving industry of brick and tile making, hence Brickmakers Lane, Brickfields and Tile Kiln Lane. The local clay made good hard bricks, forerunners of the multi-coloured Leverstock Reds later made by the Leverstock and Acorn Red Brick Company. From the village school archives of around 1840 we know that the women and children of the village also earned money by plaiting straw for the hat-making industry of Luton.

In 1800 the town of Hemel Hempstead consisted of what is now known as the 'Old Town' with five outlying hamlets, Leverstock Green being one of these. A census in 1901 shows that there were 163 inhabited houses with a population of 649. The village was divided between three parishes, namely Abbots Langley, Hemel Hempstead and St. Michaels' Rural until in 1935 it was united under the Borough of Hemel Hempstead.

The first schooling is thought to have taken place in about 1840 in a Teacher's House, built by public subscription in Bedmond Road. This building still exists and is known as 'Old School House'. The front room was used as the school and a Dame was appointed. The number of scholars increased and in 1846 a school was erected adjoining the House at a cost of £200. Education was not free, parents had to pay two pennies per week for each child until 1876 when it was lowered to one penny.

Hannah Mayhew became Headmistress in October 1871 and her diary records such comments as:

'... was quite spent' (after one week in the job!)

'William behaved so badly in dinner that I was obliged to lock him out'

'So much affected by the intensity of the cold, several of the children were quite paralysed with it'

There were some highlights, however:

'Two girls wrote what they could remember so well on their slates, that I allowed them to copy out what they had written on to paper'

'Children read XXII Revelations. A moral influence pervaded the school throughout the day – no need for corporal punishment'.

However, it all proved too much and she left after only three months!

From the early log books we find that children were kept away from school for blackberrying, bird-scaring, gleaning, weed picking, daffodilling and stone picking. Acorn gathering also brought in extra money for the families. Children were expected to plait straw at home, before and after school hours and sometimes the children plaited while sitting round the open fires in the school during oral lessons.

Despite two extensions to the existing building, numbers grew too large and in 1931 the new Church School was built in Bluebell Wood in Pancake Lane, the money being raised in various ways by the villagers, including making sweets and marmalade.

Sadly, in 1985, declining numbers of children brought about the amalgamation of the Church School with the County Primary School and the Pancake Lane site is now scheduled for redevelopment.

It is a pleasant friendly place to live with a lively community spirit. Many activities take place in the large Village Hall built in 1974 to replace the old wooden Hall which for so long had been the hub of village life.

Lilley ✑

When the non-conformist preacher John Bunyan was being persecuted it is reputed that he ministered to his hunted flock in a cellar of a 17th-century cottage in Lilley, and this must be much more than supposition, for several houses in the village were registered for worship by Protestant Dissenters.

Had Bunyan kept a diary his movements would have been more certain, but it has long been established that Bunyan had an aunt, Alice was her name, who lived in Hitchin and that he preached at Bendish and Preston, and Lilley lies on a route he could have taken from Bedford. Bunyan's hiding place in Lilley is still in existence.

Some years ago the village was honoured by a visit of the East Herts Archaeological Society. The *North Herts Mail* at the time reported:

'The party proceeded to the site of the dwelling in which Johann Kellerman, Lilley's famous alchemist, had lived in the 19th century. The party inspected the large cellar and saw the furnace which Kellerman used.'

'A neighbour entertained the visitors with an account of Kellerman's doings, handed down to her by her mother. He was, she said, very kind to the village and was approached by all in distress. On one occasion he heard that a party of gypsies, missing their way in the snow, had fallen into a dell near the turning to Lilley Hoo. Kellerman had them dug out.'

Which is a vastly different account of Kellerman's doings than the one generally known. One can only assume that later on, in his endless quest to turn base metals into gold, he lost his reason and forsook normality to live the life of a recluse.

Some others famous in history who have had connections with this small village are: Catherine Parr, the sixth wife of Henry VIII, who was a co-heiress of the village; Lord Vaux of Harrowden, Lord of Lilley Manor, who wrote the Gravedigger's Song in Hamlet; George IV as Prince Regent, who often attended the horse racing on Lilley Hoo and last, but not least, the poet, Rupert Brooke, who wrote those immortal lines:

'The Roman Road to Wendover,
By Tring and Lilley Hoo.'

Rupert Brooke was a keen walker while at Cambridge University and often walked the Icknield Way, which skirts Lilley Hoo, something else for which the village is well known.

Little Berkhamsted 🌿

The village is situated four miles west of Hertford, the county town, on high ground rising from the river Lea valley. To its east lies Bayford, and to the west is Essendon. Little Berkhamsted has been somewhat overshadowed by its much larger namesake in the west of the county. However, its history is equally as ancient and fascinating. Both derive their name from the same source: Beork, a birch tree; Hamstede, a home stead. Berkhamsted has been variously spelt Berkhamstead or Berkhampstead throughout modern times.

At the 1086 Domesday survey, the shire-moot were positive that Berchehastede (Little Berkhamsted) had belonged to Saxon kings 'as far back as they could remember', and researchers believe that the first permanent settlements were just above the Lea flood plain.

Sir Edward Denny wrote to Lord Salisbury in 1599, at the time of selling the Manors of Little Berkhamsted and Bedwell, giving him first offer of the lands. Cecil was not interested in the transaction, so in 1600 the Manor was bought by Humphrey Weld, a rich London merchant.

The New Manor, a large Victorian house, was built only a short distance from the Old Manor by John Johnson, a London building contractor. During World War Two, Captain Bertram Mills, of circus fame, lived here. He was often to be seen driving his four-in-hand coach about the lanes, complete with post-horn blowing. The house is now owned by the Rochford family.

The Rector in 1571 was Rowland Hughes, whose daughter Jane married Thomas Ken, a London attorney. Their daughter Ann was married to Isaak Walton, the *Compleat Angler*. After Jane's death, Thomas Ken re-married, and the child of this second union was born in Little Berkhamsted, and also named Thomas. This Thomas Ken was chaplain to various exalted people, including Charles II, before becoming the Bishop of Bath and Wells in 1684. He is best known as the writer of the hymns *Awake my soul and with the sun*, and the Doxology, *Glory to Thee, my God this night*.

Few villages can claim to have three rectories at one time, but this has happened in Little Berkhamsted. The present Old Rectory was built around 1737 on Robins Nest Hill, to replace the previous Tudor building. It was the residence of all rectors until 1896, when the New Rectory was built adjoining Breach Lane. This was sold as a private house, and the present Rectory is a modern bungalow in Berkampstead Lane. The Old Rectory is a well-proportioned Georgian house, the home of one Charles Johnston during the First World War. His four children were born there, and his son Brian later became the famous radio and television personality. Brian Johnston still keeps in contact with Little Berkhamsted through the Cricket Club. He wrote a delightful preface to the village history book, published by the local history group in 1981.

Nowadays, the village seems to attract pop-stars, having housed Donovan, and more recently, Adam Ant. The population of the parish has not increased as much as might be expected. In fact, the number of residents at the 1851 census was 556, ten more than in 1971. Very little new building is allowed by the Planning Authorities, as the area is designated as being one of outstanding natural beauty. For this, both residents and visitors are generally thankful.

Little Gaddesden 🦋

Little Gaddesden is an exceptionally attractive village set on a ridge 600ft up in the Chiltern Hills. Although named 'Little Gaddesden' it is in fact a long straggling village taking in the hamlets of Ringshall and Hudnall. It was probably a plague village; the church now stands alone in the fields ½ mile from the village green but there are many signs that the medieval residents originally lived in timbered huts clustered around the church.

It is impossible to describe Little Gaddesden without reference to Ashbridge House and estate. Once a monastery founded in 1285 by Edmund Plantagenet, Earl of Cornwall to house monks of the Order of Bonhommes, Ashridge became, after the Reformation, a Royal residence. It was here that in 1555 the young Princess (later Queen) Elizabeth was living when she was arrested for complicity in the Wyatt rebellion and taken to the Tower of London.

In 1605 Ashridge passed into the possession of the Egerton family, better known as the Earls and Dukes of Bridgewater. The most famous member of this family was the 3rd Duke, Francis, who succeeded in 1748. He is known as 'the Father of Inland Navigation' since he constructed one of the earliest canals in England, built to carry coal from the family's mines at Worsley in Lancashire to Manchester. The tall monument to his memory stands on the edge of an escarpment within view of Ashridge House. The present house was built by one of his successors in 1813 on the site of the monastery.

During the second half of the 19th century Lady Marion Alford, widow of Viscount Alford who had inherited the Ashridge estate, made many changes to Little Gaddesden, altering and improving the old cottages in the village. Many of them were rebuilt to her chosen designs and marked with the Alford or Brownlow symbol, sometimes with a date. Most people in the district worked on the Estate; either in the house, the gardens, the Home Farm or as gamekeepers or woodsmen; about 500–800 in all.

The Ashridge Estate's golden age under the 3rd Earl Brownlow came to an abrupt end when he died in 1921. The estate was put up for sale and its employees were given a year's wages and discharged. Many were able to buy their own cottages at a very favourable price, others had to leave the village in search of work.

111

The house was sold and became a college; during the Second World War it was a hospital. Meanwhile the land was bought for development and sold off in small plots for building. A number of new houses *were* built, mainly along the roads leading to the village and around the golf course which was laid out on part of the parkland. Thanks to the foresight of some public spirited local residents money was raised to buy a great deal of the land; woodland, parkland and downland and given to the National Trust which preserves much of this beautiful estate for all to enjoy.

Nowadays very few new houses are built owing to the restrictions on planning permission in this 'Area of Outstanding Natural Beauty'. Most residents work outside the village and many commute to London by train from Berkhamsted or Hemel Hempstead. There is a vigorous community life with 30 different clubs and societies. The oldest of these is probably the Women's Institute (founded in 1919) and the Royal British Legion. There was an Ashridge Cricket Club which played there for over a century. It moved to Little Gaddesden in 1951.

Little Hadham ❧

This attractive village is situated in the Ash Valley, surrounded by arable farmland; sheep and cows are to be seen grazing in the meadows, and farm vehicles moving around the lanes. As one walks along the village street on a warm sunny afternoon, it seems nothing has changed for a hundred years.

The name Hadham is of Anglo-Saxon origin, deriving from Hadda's Ham, the farmstead or settlement founded by Hadda, an Anglo-Saxon chieftain. Little Hadham is mentioned in the Domesday Book, when there were two manors, one held by the Bishop of London and the other by the Abbott of Ely, in 1086.

The medieval village was in the area of Church End, around the parish Church of St. Cecilia, and Stone House Farm. The farm and some of the cottages are still in existence today, but the church is no longer in the centre of the village. Settlement in the areas of the Ash and the Ford, the present-day geographical centre, date from the beginning of the 16th century.

Today Little Hadham has only one general store and Post Office, and one pub, but this was not always the case. At the beginning of the century, Houghtons, a lovely timbered house, was the general store, Post Office and bakery, with bread baked on the premises and delivered around the village. There were two butcher's shops, one of which is now an MG sports car specialist, a dairy, two sweet shops, a blacksmiths, a wheelwright, and a rushworker. At a small cottage near the ford, laundry was taken in from a large area around. One of the public houses, the Nags Head, was also a brewery.

The Nags Head is now the only remaining pub, and is very popular with visitors from all round the area. At one time there were also the Fox, the Hen and Chickens, the Angel, and the Cock, and some of these names are still preserved in the names of the houses.

During the years the village has changed very little in appearance, and picturesque houses and cottages still line the village street. At the smithy, opposite the site of the old blacksmiths, council houses have been built, and new properties have sprung up along the A120, which runs through the village. At Fordfield is a pleasant complex of flats and bungalows for the elderly of the village, the name recording the ford across the river Ash which caused many incidents of flooding before it was bridged over more than fifteen years ago.

Little Hadham provides many opportunities for its inhabitants to enjoy, both socially and in serving the community, but perhaps the greatest bonus of all is the lovely countryside all around.

Little Munden ✤

The parish is comprised of five hamlets – Dane End, Green End, Haultwick (pronounced Arctic), White Hill and Potters Green; it lies on the east Herts border midst rolling farmland. Due to the undulating countryside, narrow lanes with high banks and passing places the area is known as 'Little Devon'. Four of the five hamlets are on the hills north, east and west of the village of Dane End which lies in the valley and derives its name from the Saxon 'Dene End', meaning end of the valley.

Until the Second World War Dane End had only 26 houses, one public house, one shop and post office and the forge. These still remain, and the forge now sells petrol from pumps which are still worked by hand. After the 1939-45 War, land was bought by the then Ware District Council for Council dwellings. This was followed by the sale of Dane End House estate to a private developer, and Dane End was aptly known as the 'mushroom village', and is now a popular village for commuters to London, Hatfield, Luton, Stevenage and to the local towns of Ware and Hertford.

The Dane End Estate passed through many hands until the early 19th century when Nathaniel and Charles Chauncey lived at Green End House and Dane End House respectively. These two houses were passed by direct descent to the Gladstone family. In 1916 Herbert Gladstone, the youngest son of William Gladstone P.M., retired as Governor General of South Africa and took up residence at Dane End House until his death in 1930. He was a popular figure in the village, loved by everyone, and known to all as 'Lordy'.

Decendants of his widow sold the estate in the early 1960s – property and farms being sold individually, altering the whole character of the village.

So we see the growth in housing from sixty to three hundred and sixty in the span of twenty-five years – the larger proportion of the building has taken place in the Dane End valley. Now Dane End is the largest of the hamlets whereas for centuries it was the smallest.

Little Munden Church dates from 1100 and stands on a hill overlooking the village of Dane End. In the churchyard there is an ancient yew tree, now sadly only half the original size due to high gales in February, 1980.

Visitors to Little Munden may have difficulty in locating it for it cannot be found on maps or signposts. Little Munden proper is All Saints Church, Primary School, School House, Rectory and Lordship Farm and lies in the centre of the parish. In the early 20th century no less than seven roads and footpaths led to the centre of the parish.

But Little Munden went off the map when the G.P.O. gave the new postal address and telephone exchange as Dane End. Thankfully the church and school, Rectory, School House and Lordship Farm still retain the old English name – and long may it remain.

London Colney 🦢

Isolated now and bounded by trunk roads leading to what present-day planners believe to be more important centres, the heart of the village – 'Coney Green' as it appears on early maps – was once on the main route from London to Holyhead. It provided a respite for coaches and travellers of all kinds with a good quantity of inns with stabling accommodation; The Swan, George, Bull and Butcher (now all demolished) and Green Dragon and Bull, all clustered round the ford through the river Colne, vying for custom. Those were indeed busy days!

To help the travellers continue their journeys more easily and safely, a bridge was built beside the ford by the St. Albans and South Mimms Turnpike Trust in 1773. It was designed and built by local folk – those searching for links between such an attractive bridge with its seven arches and the famous Thomas Telford, are disappointed!

Sadly included in the minutes of the Trust, a couple of years later is included the legend, 'Some evil dispos'd Person or Persons had destroyed some of the Stone Coping from the bridge at London Colney.' Vandals then, as now, maybe.

However, the bridge stood the test of time, despite a motor lorry crashing through the parapet on one occasion, and it was not until the late 1940s that the authorities decided that the width of the bridge was inadequate for the motor traffic and that something must be done to remedy the situation. Therefore the stone parapets were removed and white painted iron railings substituted, while the original arches, strengthened with buttresses, remained.

The banks of the river were criss-crossed with paths and tracks and were unkempt and unattractive. The larger expanse was occasionally used for village festivities – fairs and the like, and there is a delightful record in *The Statesman* of 1814 of the celebrations held in '... the Tranquil village of London Colney' upon the capture of Napoleon.

Eventually in the early 1960s, the local council claimed the northern bank of the river stretching as far as the road in front of the Green Dragon public house as Common land, and proceeded to landscape the area, planting it with trees and bulbs, some of which were donated by a local firm who used the local hostelries to entertain business visitors.

Consequently the local inhabitants, who had previously been active in the upkeep of their own properties were encouraged by the council's attentions and as a result the riverside area has been designated of special interest. The oldest buildings still surviving are the Green Dragon, The Bull, and Waterside House – the half-timbered house on the south bank of the river.

For many years, between Waterside and Broad Colney, gravel had been extracted from the riverside area. This part has been developed into a Nature Reserve including lakes which abound with all kinds of wildlife, and which are administered by the Herts and Middlesex Nature Conservancy Trust. Car parking is free at Broad Colney, Shenley Lane, and a pleasant time can be had exploring the whole area.

London Colney village has changed dramatically from the small nucleus of dwellings around the green and straggling for a short distance along the road to St. Albans, which is all that appears on the maps at the turn of this century, when it catered for a population of about 900.

Some council and private housing was erected in about 1928 and shortly afterwards, but it was not until after the Second World War that the majority of houses were built, catering for all needs. Such development is continuing today, although not at such a pace. The population now stands at about 12,000!

There has been controversy over the infiltration into the middle of the village of warehouses and industries which encourage the modern heavy lorry into the mainly residential areas. In the meantime, we continue to care for our village green and our surroundings and hope to encourage more people to share in our appreciation of a beautiful piece of Hertfordshire's rural history.

Maple Cross 🍁

Its name is thought to have come from the maypole dancing, as in 1588 it was recorded that the local village of Mill End complained of the noise to the Lord of the Manor.

The Cross Inn is 17th century and once had a blacksmith's shop next door, also a row of cottages called Yew Tree Cottages. These were pulled down after the Second World War and three shops were built, but the yew trees remain.

Maple Cross in the early 1900s had only farms and farm cottages, but over the years houses have been built, privately and council owned and now there are about 800 houses in the village.

The Community Centre is used by the village for the Women's Institute, Guides, Brownies, Over 60s, fishing club and various other activities. The Cubs have their own hall.

The Industrial estate is on the north of the village and covers acres which used to be Little Farm Field. There are about 16 factories on the site producing a variety of goods for home and export.

The unused gravel diggings to the east of the village are now being made into nature reserves, boating and fishing lakes. It is encouraging the wildlife, especially the wild birds. The Canadian Geese have made the lakes their home over the last 10 years and during the summer mornings and evenings are a fine sight flying in formation to look for food on the local fields.

Mardley Heath ✣

Mardley Heath, a settlement to the north of Welwyn is a growing community, mirrored on the east of the Great North Road by Oaklands. New developments are surrounded by roads with such romantic names, redolent of the highwayman, as Turpin's Ride, Hangman's Lane and Robbery Bottom Lane. Recently the Scouts, with much support from the community in general, built the Elizabeth of Glamis Hall, now used to capacity by the youth of the district.

Although Mardley Heath has few of the traditional constituents of a village, its increasing population may soon turn its desire for a separate identity into a reality.

Markyate ✣

The village seems to have derived its trade for several centuries from the sale of provisions and other necessaries useful to travellers passing along Watling Street who found it a convenient half way house between St. Albans and Dunstable; it is highly probable that a kind of market was established here for the convenience of travellers. During the middle of the 18th century the Industrial Revolution was taking place. Better roads were needed for quicker transportation and the stage coach system was set up. The basis for this system were the inns along the route which provided for change of horses and food and accommodation for the passengers. Being astride the Watling Street, Markyate became one of the staging posts from London to the north west. Five such coaching inns were listed in Pigots Directory of 1839. In 1900 there were 13 inns and public houses in the village but as at 1986 there are only 4 remaining.

Part of Markyate's history is connected with the famous carrier firm of Pickfords who started their business in the mid 17th century with the use of pack horses and who a century later were able to advertise that they could move goods from Manchester to London in $4\frac{1}{2}$ days.

The principal historic interest of Markyate centres round The Cell. The present Manor House is built upon the site of an ancient Priory and was purchased in 1548 by George Ferrers and was in the Ferrers family until 1660, just over 100 years. During this time Kathleen Ferrers, the infamous Wicked Lady of Markyate Cell, was pursuing her notorious calling of highway robber. Born in 1634, she was married at the age of 14 to a 16 year old member of the aristocracy. The marriage was not a success and as an escape from the boring life at the Cell she turned to highway robbery. At night she changed into her three cornered hat, breeches and cloak and mounted her coal black horse with pistols at her waist and set off to hold up the long-distance coaches which travelled the Watling Street.

One night during one of these hold-ups she was shot at and seriously wounded but managed to get back to the Cell where she collapsed and died near the door of the secret room which she used as her hide-away. The family tried to hush up the cause of her death, a false statement was issued and she was buried with ceremony that befitted her rank and status. It was hoped that her death and all the rumours that were being circulated in the countryside would soon be forgotten. This however was not to be. Curious stories of the Wicked Lady's ghost which was said to appear near the Cell and travellers on the Watling Street saw her riding in the lanes and soon all local mishaps including a fire at the Cell itself were put down to her evil influence. So the legend of Kathleen Ferrers, the Wicked Lady of Markyate Cell has been kept alive for the past 300 years.

In 1955 the work on the bypass began. A new road $1\frac{1}{4}$ miles long was constructed to avoid the narrow dangerous Markyate High Street which was the only public highway in the country to have a 15 m.p.h. speed limit. The opening of the bypass in 1957 greatly relieved the congestion of traffic in the High Street and also with the building of the M1 motorway Markyate Village has become a thriving community and a desirable, pleasant village in which to live.

Meesden 🌿

Meesden is a very small village; only 100 adults. Most now work away, but originally men were woodcutters, gamekeepers or farm workers. The manor was the home of Baron and Baroness Dimsdale. (His ancestor was a doctor and in gratitude for inoculation against smallpox, Catherine the Great of Russia gave him a barony and a sum of money.) The manor was completely destroyed by a doodlebug in the 1939-45 war.

Meesden fair was held every May, opposite the Fox, this was a great event for the farmers and all the families around.

The deer are often seen in Scales Wood and the fields around. Some of the old grassland has never been ploughed or sprayed and many different species of wild flowers can be found.

The church is hidden away in a wood up a long rough track, in 1086 it belonged to the Bishop of London. The south porch is of 16th-century brick work. There is an impressive monument to Robert Younger, a benefactor who left the pasture known as Town Close to the village. This was sold, and every Christmas interest on the money is given to the widows and pensioners of Meesden. Meesden Hall, a lovely Queen Anne House is no longer the rectory, but the church remains loved and cared for by the present inhabitants of Meesden.

Much Hadham 🌿

This village is a straggling delightful place lying in the valley of the river Ash.

The fact that many of its houses are Tudor, several are Georgian, and there is only a sprinkling of more modern homes, tells the visitor that the settlement is an ancient one. Indeed, we probably owe the name to Hadda, a Saxon warrior successful in a battle which took place against the Danes outside Widford.

The earliest written records are to be found in the will of a Saxon Queen and dated 946 A.D. Childless, she left her lands in Hadham to the Bishops of London. Thus it was that the first to inherit built himself a summer palace in the village while, at the same time, avoiding the plague-ridden crowded capital.

When nearly 500 years later, Katharine, widow of Henry V, was placed in the custody of the Bishop of London, he dispatched her to his summer palace and there she gave birth to Edmund, her son by Owen Tudor, Clerk of her Wardrobe. Edmund in due course had a son – later to become Henry VII – so Much Hadham can claim to have nourished the founder of the Tudor dynasty.

People come and people go, and those who left under the threat of religious persecution founded Haddam, Connecticut in 1662. Three hundred years later, people from Hadham, England, travelled to the United States to take part in the tercentenary celebrations and friendships made then flourish still.

Nowadays in Much Hadham the spirit of ecumenism is abroad and the Anglican and Roman Catholic communities are very close. From the proceeds of the sale of land owned by the local Roman Catholics, in 1978 a Health Centre was built, and opened by Cardinal Hume.

In 1983, the congregations of St. Andrew's and The Church of the Holy Cross came together to share, very happily, the Parish Church.

Nash Mills 🥀

Nash Mill, from which ιne village takes its name, was converted to paper making in the 18th century. It was bought by John Dickinson in 1811. He was the founder of the well-known firm of Paper Makers and Manufacturing Stationers, John Dickinson & Co. Ltd. He lived with his wife in Nash House, a pleasant house in the mill grounds, which is now used as offices for the mill.

By the early 1800s the Grand Junction Canal had been constructed through this area, its course passing by Nash Mills taking in the waters of the river Gade for some distance. The canal was well used for over a century to transport goods and supplies to and from the mills. Incidentally, most of the working narrow boats have now been converted for use as holiday homes afloat, and the canal is still much used for this purpose.

At the time of the introduction of the Uniform Penny Post by Rowland Hill in 1840, Dickinsons were producing at Nash Mills a very special paper which had silk threads running through it. This paper was chosen for the first official postal cover or envelope called 'the Mulready'. The paper was also used for

Exchequer Bonds and important documents as a safeguard against forgery.

John Dickinson moved from Nash House in 1839 to a new house he had built on a nearby hill. The house he called Abbots Hill and it is now an exclusive private school. One of his partners, John Evans who was married to John Dickinson's youngest daughter, later moved into Nash House. John Evans was an outstanding Archaeologist and Numismatist. He held many important offices and was, like John Dickinson, a Fellow of the Royal Society. He was created a Knight Commander of the Bath in 1892. Many well known people visited him at Nash House, one of whom was Captain Scott who came to discuss with Sir John, who was Treasurer of the Royal Society, the financing of his expedition to the South Pole.

The village school at Nash Mills was built by John Dickinson in 1847 for the education of his apprentices and the village children. It is still in use, as is adjacent School House, but with some modern extensions. Up to 1891, when elementary education became free, Nash Mills' parents still had to contribute pence to help pay for the education of their children at this school. Some Government grants were then available but they largely depended on regular attendance and standards attained. Government Inspectors visited the schools to assess these. The school is now Nash Mills Church of England School, being now in the Ecclesiastical Parish of Apsley. In Nash Mills there is a Wesleyan Methodist Church, but the C. of E. church is St. Mary's, at Apsley.

Northaw 🌿

Northaw Women's Institute is the oldest in Hertfordshire, founded in November 1917. Its unbroken history is recorded in minute books and other papers which are kept in the County Archives. It is interesting to read what the institute did during its early days. One early happening was the purchase of a suction sweeper – the forerunner of today's vacuum cleaner, which members could hire for 6d. (old pence) per day. Another was making slippers for the village children to wear in school to avoid them sitting all day in wet shoes when the weather was bad. Setting up a glove-making industry from rabbit skins, making jam for hospitals and digging for victory are all recorded in these books.

There are still many working farms in Northaw predominantly sheep and arable. One spectacular sight is the herd of Highland cattle at Park Farm; and in springtime the flock of sheep with their lambs at Colesdale Farm are a delight to young and old. As well as sheep, the fields of Colesdale Farm are now witness to sights never seen in the past; namely micro-light aircraft, which on still weekends take to the sky and buzz overhead like pterodactyls from prehistoric times. These same fields are also the setting for the Enfield Chace Point to Point which takes place every year, on a usually chilly spring bank holiday. It is run on the old original Northaw race course. Not an Epsom type course – but an old route over the fields, which just has the local name of 'race course'.

For over 50 years the Greyhound Racing Association had kennels at The Hook Northaw. Here at their peak they employed a community of approximately 200 workers to look after about 750 dogs. On racing days the large vans could be seen transporting the dogs to the White City. In 1985 the kennels closed, now the houses and kennels are empty and parts of the estate have been sold.

There are many walks and footpaths in Northaw which reflect the beauty of the Hertfordshire countryside. Northaw Great Wood is a well-known feature and is the remains of the original Enfield Chace, which was a scrubland area extending from Hatfield to Enfield and was the royal hunting ground of James I. Northaw was in the centre of this area and the old cottages at Northaw, Newgate Street and Castle Farm were built for the men servants to sleep in; and the great manor houses of Theobalds Park, Nyn Park and elsewhere were built for the nobility and gentry who hunted here. Now owned and maintained by Hertfordshire County Council it is a very fine recreational area, provided with ample car parking and has planned and routed walks for all to enjoy. It has a wealth of wildlife and is a delight for naturalists. A woodland paradise, it can be enjoyed by all whatever the season, be it spring with the bluebells, the hot days of summer, mists of autumn or frosts and snow of winter. There is always something different to see. If you are really lucky you may catch a glimpse of a Muntjac deer hiding in the bushes, a fox slinking through the bracken or a rabbit running for safety.

Although the roar of London traffic is clearly audible during weekday rush hours, and the lights of the M25 motorway are now visible at night, those living in Northaw are privileged to live in a truly rural environment. Part of the green belt and a conservation area, Northaw will hopefully remain a village for many years to come, in spite of the pressures now being put on the countryside surrounding London.

Northchurch ॐ

The centre of village life is the Parish Church of St. Mary which has a history going back to Saxon times and the church typifies the continuous life of the village over many centuries. A point of interest in the history of the church is that the churchyard contains the grave of one, Peter the Wild Boy, who died in 1785. He was brought to England on the instructions of Queen Caroline in 1725 after he had been found wandering, almost wild, in a forest in Germany. He was looked after by a Northchurch farmer and, in view of his wandering nature, a collar was placed around his neck giving his address. This collar is still in existence and is in Berkhamsted School. Another interesting point is the flag which hangs inside the church and which was a gift from H.R.H. Prince of Wales. The royal connection with the church arises from the fact that the advowson remained vested in the Prince of Wales as Duke of Cornwall when the large area known as the Ashridge Estate (now part of the National Trust property) was sold to Lord Brownlow.

The village itself has changed immeasurably since the end of the Second World War and has almost entirely been redeveloped leaving very few of the older premises in being. The most interesting of the remaining older buildings (15th/16th century) are the George and Dragon P.H. the Church Almshouses, Arne House, Dudswell, Dudswell House, Rosemary Cottage and Dropshort Cottage. Rosemary Cottage, abutting the A41, has at varying times been a farmhouse, a tobacco warehouse and a laundry. A cottage, No. 7 Bell Lane was once used as a straw plaiting school for local children and a mantelpiece was carved with plait measurements. The plait was sent to Luton for use in the straw hat industry.

These changes have not affected the spirit of the village or its inhabitants, newcomers though many of them are, and there is a strong sense of community as is indicated by the fact that the village W.I. has recently compiled a list giving details of no less than 35 organisations of every sort which are vigorously active in the village. These lists are distributed to all new arrivals by W.I. members.

Offley ❧

The village lies on the edge of the Chilterns on top of a 1 in 8 hill from the Hitchin side, it is in the centre of fertile farms and beautiful woods. The Icknield Way separates it from the Parish of Pirton to the north and is a beautiful walk via the hamlet of Wellbury.

We count ourselves lucky in Offley that we still have a school, a church (though no longer a resident vicar) a village shop and Post Office and a local butcher who has a fund of jokes he readily embarks on when selling you his fine meat.

We have a better bus service than many villages, mainly because we lie on the road between Hitchin and Luton, but this has been drastically reduced during the last few years. This is partly because a fine new road was built, called Offley Bypass as part of the A505 on the stretch from Hitchin to Luton. This was a great blessing to the village in as much as it removed a large volume of traffic from the road that cuts the village in two and often made it too busy for pedestrians to cross for several minutes at a time; but the sting in the tail was that half the buses were put on the by-pass and called express 'flyers' to the great disgust of the villagers of Offley and Lilley who wondered where all the travellers would come from who would need to do this journey at the great saving of about five minutes!

However, amongst our other blessings we count regular milk and newspaper deliveries, a fish and chip van twice a week, a wet-fish seller once a week and a sturdy character called Mr. Spencer who calls with paraffin, calor gas, hardware and gardening accessories and almost aything else that a housewife would dread running out of. No inclement weather has been known to stop him and if he should get delayed by snow and ice you may find him at your door after 10 p.m. still working, or early the next day, full of apologies.

Offley is not as picturesque as some English villages but is in the Green Belt in an area of outstanding natural beauty. There are several large old houses with mainly Georgian or Queen Anne

125

facades, several of the inns are at least four hundred years old but have been altered and extended and several older houses have been refurbished, mainly tastefully.

There are a large number of council houses which replaced tiny agricultural workers' cottages to begin with and then extended the numbers of houses. These estates are pleasantly bordered with trees and wide grass verges and are often mixed in or near the private housing, which helps to form a more integrated community than is found in other places. Most people travel to work, but with Hitchin and Luton so near, it has not become a purely dormitory village. Many newcomers have arrived during the last twenty years to what was rather a closed community with many village families related to each other by blood or marriage. House prices have soared and it is difficult for young people to get housing, but an amazing number of young marrieds do wait on the housing list and stay in the village or return here after a short interval away.

While young people still want to live in a village and the school is open and successful, the community will survive.

Old Hatfield

With a thriving jet aircraft and aerodynamics industry lying alongside the busy A1 motorway which is a goodly portion of boundary on one side, and a fast rail link with London and the North as another, the larger part of Hatfield is sandwiched between the two and is known as New Town, but on the 'other side of the track' is a much older part of Hatfield known as Old Hatfield. This then we call our village.

Opposite the entrance to the rail station are a pair of fine gates with a Statue of the 3rd Marquess of Salisbury, who served three times in the office of Prime Minister to Queen Victoria and it is his family who have been so prominent in Hatfield's life through the years. Centuries before it was known as Haethfield and the Saxon King Edgar in the 10th century gave land to the Monks of Ely, and subsequently Cardinal Morton built a palace in the area when he was chief minister of Henry 7th, it being in the diocese of Ely. It was in a part of this palace where Elizabeth Tudor was imprisoned by her half-sister Mary and where she heard the news that she was to succeed her and become Queen Elizabeth I; she chose Lord

Burghley as her chief minister who remained loyal to her for 40 years, but it was his son Robert Cecil who was to make his mark in Hatfield by exchanging the Cecil home at Theobalds in South Hertfordshire with King James I, because the King preferred it to the old monastery.

So in 1607 the Cecils were firmly established in Hatfield when Robert built Hatfield House the family home which has stood atop the hill since completion in 1611, and is probably the largest attraction in Hatfield with its fine pictures, especially the 'Rainbow Portrait' of Elizabeth I. There is a fine Jacobean staircase which incorporates carvings of John Tradescant, the Royal gardener who introduced several plants into this country, and after whom is named the trailing plant Tradescantia. There are several tapestries and those known as the 'Four Seasons' are English, woven by the Sheldon family and being the most notable, hang in the armoury alongside the beautiful marble hall with its minstrel gallery and fine painted ceiling: one could spend hours admiring the many treasures of this fine house or rather home for it is still lived in by the family of the 6th Marquess and Marchioness of Salisbury.

There is still part of the Old Palace remaining which is now a Banqueting Hall open most evenings for Elizabethan style dinners, the accompanying music and entertainment being of the same period attracts people from all over the world, its setting being so true: the whole is set in vast parkland with farms, saw mills, and cattle grazing close to the many lovely walks criss–crossing the estate. These too are open to the public to enjoy in the fair seasons. Until recent years one could also watch cricket on the lawn to the rear of the house, but due to increasing numbers of visitors who might fall prey to a 'boundary 6' the venue was moved elsewhere in the town, quite a loss of tradition to the older inhabitants of Old Hatfield.

Most of the old shops and buildings in Old Hatfield have either gone or been updated and a fine new set of smart buildings and Georgian style residences has grown up around the quadrangle known as Salisbury Square. Some of the shopkeepers still bear the name from past generations who had connections with this small area for over a century. Gray's garage is one such family name, their premises have dodged about from one spot to another as the old town developed.

Old Stevenage

The days have long since gone when Stevenage was a village centred around the old parish church of St. Nicholas. The old town is now part of the thriving Borough of Stevenage, one of the post war New Towns.

The High Street has retained much of its old world charm, this wide thoroughfare once part of the Great North Road, with scenes in the past of busy coaching days, and much later modern day traffic.

Running parallel with the High Street is Middle Row, with its collection of small shops and businesses, including a jewellers, shoe repairers and hairdressers. Middle Row is reputed to be the site of the Annual Charter Fair, dating back 700 years. The Charter was granted by Edward I in 1281 and every year at the end of September the Fair has been held in the High Street, which is closed to traffic. It is a very colourful sight to see.

At the end of Middle Row stands the Old Castle Inn, better known these days as the Nat West Bank. In the rafters at the rear of the building rests the coffin of one Henry Trigg, it was placed there according to the directions in his will, to thwart the body-snatchers of his day.

Samuel Pepys the diarist was one of the more famous travellers to visit Stevenage. He and his wife stayed at the Old Swan Inn, better known today as the Registry Office, and whilst staying there played bowls on the green opposite. The Swan Inn was reputed to be the first stopping place for young couples on their way to Gretna Green.

Stevenage has a great sense of history, possibly the coaching era being the greatest, when 20 coaches or more travelled through daily with services to Edinburgh, Carlisle and Glasgow. Some of the Inns that serviced these coaches still remain today and offer the same service and friendliness as in the past.

Panshanger

The following lines were written about the famous Panshanger Oak around 1824: 'This celebrated tree stands in the pleasure grounds of the Right Honourable Earl Cowper's mansion at

Panshanger. It is, I believe the largest oak in the Country, and is known throughout England on account of its size and vigour of its growth.

A measurement of this tree was made in the year 1719, when it was found to contain 315 cubic feet of good timber. And again, in the year 1805 (29th May) under the direction of the fifth Earl Cowper, Mr. Edward Ellis of Hertford, made another measurement and found the tree contained 796 cubic fee, including the branches considered of sufficient size to be timber. From this statement we glean that in 86 years the Panshanger Oak had increased its bulk to over double, viz 481 cubic feet. We also know that 169 years ago it contained 315 cubic feet of timber. In George Strutt's *Sylva Brittanica* (published 1826) there is a fine plate (iv) drawn and etched by the author, of this tree. The engraving shows the tree surrounded by shrubs and in full leaf. Mr. Strutt gives the following information respecting it: 'This elegant tree according to tradition was known as The Great Oak of Panshanger for more than a century ago; it appears however, even now to have scarcely reached its prime; the waving lightness of its feathered branches dipping down towards its stem to the very ground, the straightness of its trunk, and the redundancy of its foliage, all give it a character opposite to that of antiquity, and fit it for the cultivated and sequestered pleasure grounds belonging to the mansion of Earl Cowper at Panshanger, Hertford, where it stands surrounded with evergreens and lighter shrubs, of which it seems at once the guardian and the pride. It contains one thousand feet of timber, and its nineteen feet of circumference at three feet from the ground.'

The poet Cowley in one of his poems exclaims, 'Hail old patrician trees.' Surely this grand tree is worthy of some such exclamation, for has it not for many years kept silent watch over the 'House of Panshanger'.

Park Street ✑

It was the Saxons who first developed a village here. Two mills for grinding corn were built on the river. Both still stand, but Park Mill has had many uses in its time. The most recent was for storing junk and scrap. It is shortly to be converted into offices. The other, Moor Mill, is shortly to be made into a restaurant and motel.

129

The Romans built Watling Street which runs straight through the village. When St. Alban was martyred in 209 A.D. the road was used by pilgrims travelling to worship at his shrine. The pilgrims had a very hazardous journey, as robbers and murderers abounded and preyed on them. One of the buildings in the village was used as a lodging house for them, and still exists. It was at one time two labourers' cottages. Later it became a shop. This building is known affectionately locally as 'Duck your nut' because of its very low doorway. Our forbears must have been very small people. Another old building is Toll Cottage in Bury Dell Lane. This once housed a recruiting officer for Cromwell's army.

Hyde Lane and Burston Drive are two very old roads in the locality. When gravel workers took over land adjoining Hyde Lane in 1943 the foundations of a Roman villa were unearthed, and nearby, two stone coffins containing skeletons of a man and a woman. These are now in Verulamium Museum. Here too were found the remains of a hospital for infectious diseases, built at the time of the Black Death in 1349. It was later used for the withdrawal of suspect cattle, and a slaughter house. Burston Drive was a continuation of Hyde Lane and led to Burston Manor which was a farm dating back to Roman days. This house is one of the few examples of moated manors still in existence, although part of the moat has since been filled in. A Roman kiln was unearthed at nearby Mayflower Road. It was excavated by an archaeological society. They photographed it and then covered it in.

At that time, there were several tributaries of the Ver which were wide and deep enough to float rafts, on which were carried tiles from the kiln to a wharf in the village.

The village church, Holy Trinity, was built in 1842. There was found to be still so much water 2 feet down, that the adjoining land could not be used for burials. It was not drained sufficiently until fifty years later.

The river Ver, on its way from St. Albans to join the river Colne, passes through the village. At a point near the present railway station it is joined by one of its tributaries. This secondary stream was used for many years as watercress beds. It became a very lucrative business until very recently. The railway, built in 1857, helped considerably by carrying the cress far and near particularly to London.

1930 saw the beginning of the industrial estate of Park Street. Farmland was sold, and Handley Page, the aeronautical firm, moved in. All the land on the eastern side of Watling Street up to the main railway line was taken over for hangars and the airfield. This gave work for many people and new houses sprang up for them. The peace of the village was soon shattered. Airplanes were taken out on to the airfield, and engines revved up for testing. Experimental flights zoomed overhead. Now Handley Page has gone. The hangars, divided into smaller units, are factories and offices. The airfield remains. Many proposals have been made; a leisure area, a self-contained village . . . buts it waits still for the powers in charge to make up their minds.

The old Watling Street, once the A5 is now the A5128, and endless streams of traffic pass through. Juggernauts, lorries to and from the industrial estate, commuters' cars, every possible kind of vehicle form traffic jams at peak hours. However, we do have a pelican crossing to enable us to cross safely. This was finally installed after much pressure from all the village organisations.

The Pelhams ✺

In the north-eastern corner of the county lie The Pelhams, set on a low plateau cut by streams into an attractive rolling landscape. Arable farming predominates with field colours changing dramatically through the year from the brown of winter and the green and gold of grain to the vivid yellow of the rape crop. The only large estate (about one thousand acres) belongs to Furneux Pelham Hall. Here a herd of deer provides venison for market. Partridge and pheasant are afforded ample cover in the mixed woodland plantations, created by P.O.W.s during the 1939–45 war. These trees add interest to what might otherwise have become an unbroken vista of great open fields, many hedgerows having disappeared in the cause of higher grain production.

There is a mixture of dwellings of all ages in each village, timber-framed or modern brick, some tiled, others thatched. Many are rented from farmers, the council or the local brewery; others are owner-occupied. They are scattered quite thinly along lanes, the two villages virtually merging.

At the eastern end of Stocking Pelham, on the highest land and standing athwart the Essex border is the C.E.G.B. grid station. Pylons and cables radiate in all directions but trees have been planted and will grow in time to improve the outlook. The Pelhams

131

Field Study Centre, situated here and visited by countless school-children, testifies to the lack of disturbance caused to the natural environment.

Stocking Pelham (pop. 132) has a focal centre – a road junction where the thatched and weatherboarded Cock public house stands. Just a few yards away is the Victorian school building which served its original purpose from 1874–1918. It has been enlarged and is used as a village hall, where each day the walls still echo with the voices of children – those attending the playgroup and toddlers club.

The little church, standing in a round churchyard about half a mile to the west, is mostly 14th century, though it is believed to be on the site of a Saxon chapel.

From Duck Street in the west, for two miles, sprawl the scattered houses of Furneux Pelham. East End existed almost as a separate entity until this century. It has a dozen houses and three farms. The population has contracted, for many of the cottages once housing several families have been converted into single dwellings. There were shops here within living memory but none are left today.

At Barleycroft End crossroads stands The Brewery Tap public house and Rayments Brewery. The brewery, now part of Greene King, still brews the famous BBA and employs over fifty people. William Rayment began brewing whilst living at The Hall, but built maltings at the present site in 1860. The water supply comes from its own artesian well. Though the brewery was always a going concern, renewed interest in 'real ale' has stimulated business, and a bigger fermentation vessel has been installed. On brewing days a strong malty smell wafts over the village.

Past the brewery flows the river Ash, a tributary of the Lea. It is a silted, sluggish stream which suddenly swells into a deep torrent after rain. Running northwards is Violets Lane, luring the unwary visitor, for it is marked on most maps. The notice warning of a 'Ford' is misleading, as the road actually runs along the bed of the Ash for a mile!

The rather unsightly village hall, little used now, despite a population of well over four hundred, is a reminder of days when the village was a closer-knit community of souls. It has a recent extension to accommodate a consultation room for twice-weekly doctors' visits. Next door stood the last shop in Furneux Pelham, closed in the late 1970s and converted into a house.

The same fate befell the old school built in the Victorian age but quite tastefully adapted. Nearby, the educational needs of today's infant and junior children are better catered for in a suitably designed modern building.

It is difficult for the fairweather visitor to judge village life here. The beauty of the landscape and tranquil aspect are striking, but winter can be a grim, grimy battle with mud and flooded or snowbound roads. In the past this was even more of a problem for now better roads and drainage mean better communication. Village life and villagers themselves have changed vastly in the last forty years. Agriculture for example is no longer labour-intensive: each of the dwindling number of farms employs two or three men instead of twenty or more. One source of local employment is the brewery; other men have practical occupations like plumbing, building or electrical work which can be put to use in the area. Many commute as far as London and thus have little spare time or interest to form social roots in the community. A good number of women work too and have less time to participate in village activities, which used to bind people together.

Transport has provided the means of 'escape', opening up options for outside entertainment that would have been catered for in the village say before the last war. This is not necessarily a bad thing, but not all are fortunate enough to own cars so some are now deprived of social contact as village-centred life declines. Children in particular can suffer and parents with transport can spend hours taking their children to leisure activities or education classes in larger towns.

The enlargement of Stansted Airport, a contentious issue, will, apart from increased noise, ring even greater changes. Already there is pressure to 'urbanise' the villages. House prices are set to rise enormously, thus forcing out relatively poorer paid but long-established families. Furneux and Stocking Pelham are likely to be torn in the conflict between the preservation of the traditional village community with close relationships and loyalties and the desperate need for rejuvenation and revitalisation if the decline in the quality of village life is to be reversed.

Pirton 🦜

The fear of fire destroying life, home and possessions is very real, but how much greater must have been the dread some 100 years ago when many buildings were thatched and the only water supply came from the village ponds and wells – and these were often low in the summertime. There was no telephone and the only means of getting a message to Hitchin for the fire brigade was a journey of some 3½ miles either on foot or by horse. The village people had to be extremely self-reliant. This story tells of fires caused by a thunderstorm, with catastrophic results.

On Thursday, 20th May 1895, a thunderstorm which passed over Pirton left one man dead, another severely injured, and burnt down four cottages, leaving families homeless and destroying furniture and possessions.

At an inquest into the death of George Downham which was held in the Royal Oak public house in Pirton before Mr. F. Shillitoe, the Coroner. A verdict of 'Accidental Death' was returned and the full story of the calamity emerged. Abraham Weeden, Daniel Goldsmith, Arthur Smith and the deceased were working for Mr. King, carting wheat from a stack in Low Field, Pirton, to the threshing machine at Holwell. About 3 p.m. the thunderstorm broke and they took shelter against another stack where they were joined by John Weeden and James Baines. There was a crash of thunder, but the witness saw no lightning, and all the men fell down. The witness, Abraham Weeden, said he rolled over three times, got up, but felt numb in his legs. The other men did not get up. By this time the stack was well on fire. He pulled the men away except the deceased, whom he could not move, then went for help. William Walker came and was joined by Frank Day, a bricklayer, and together they pulled the dead man away. He was dreadfully burnt, his features being quite unrecognisable. The handle of his pocket knife was charred almost to ashes but his watch, although discoloured, went for another half hour. He was aged about 40 years, lived at Holwell, and was married with two children.

At about the same time as the stack was set on fire, a thatched cottage some 500 yards away was struck by lightning. No-one was home at the time, the tenant Mr. John Pearce being at work, and his wife happened to be out. The cottage was soon alight and burned rapidly. John Thrussell at once drove off to Hitchin to alert the fire brigade. Eight minutes after the message was received, the brigade was on its way, under Captain Logsden and Lieutenant Barham. Although there was a steam pump, the equipment was horse-drawn and, with the torrential rain, the road to Pirton was at one point two feet under water, so deep that it put out the fire in the steam pump. Incidentally, there was not a drop of rain at Hitchin.

In the meantime the fire had spread to the adjoining cottages. Mr. W. Newberry climbed onto the beams and directed neighbours to hand up buckets of water to help check the fire until the fire engine arrived. John Pearce lost all his furniture, as did his neighbours, the Roberts brothers, who unfortunately were both deaf and dumb. From the third cottage, the home of Thomas Baines, furniture was removed. The bustle and excitement can be imagined as neighbours and others worked with a will to save whatever they could. By the time the fire engine arrived, all they could do was prevent the fire from spreading to the entire row of homes. This they managed to do with much willing help, and water taken from a nearby pond. So ended a day of drama and sadness. The fire brigade left at 9 p.m. with men on watch for any further damage either at the cottages or the stacks, but the night remained quiet with no wind, and all was well.

None of the occupants were insured although the owner, Mrs. Phoebe Davies, was. Great was the sympathy of all the villagers. It was a heavy loss for people of such slender means.

A subscription list was opened by Mr. Davies, the Guardian of the Poor of Pirton, and Superintendent Reynolds of Hitchin Police, for contributions – however small – to help those who had lost property in the fire and to be shared by the relatives of the men killed in the storm and the injured.

Potten End ✑

Potten End lies at the eastern end of the Chilterns and borders on beautiful National Trust country, including the Ashridge estate and Berkhamsted Common.

At 525 ft. it is considerably colder and windier than the neighbouring towns, a fact well known to local gardeners. The present-day village grew up in the mid 19th century. At first it comprised a compact group of cottages called The Front, The Back and The Square together with Nursery Terrace, also a few individual houses of a much earlier date, and a scattering of farms and their attendant cottages.

The present population is made up of people in all walks of life; some born in the village and living here all their lives, others having evacuated from London during the 1939–45 war who decided to stay. Some settled here due either to the easy commuting distance to London or their connection with the nearby Wellcome Foundation.

Some cottages were built in the 19th century by Lord Brownlow's Ashridge Estate, and in the early 20th century by two benefactors, Miss Sydney Courtauld and Mr. Spencer Holland; these were modernised when main drainage came to the village in the early 1960s.

Miss Courtauld built, and lived in, a fine house call Bocking, later to be called Bullbeggars by the Cooper family, famous originally for inventing sheep dip and later for aerosol sprays.

Potten End became a centre of market gardening in the early part of this century when Lane's Nurseries extended over nearly the whole of the village. They were famous for fruit trees (Lane's Prince Albert), Rhododendrons and conifers and many fine specimens of these still exist in the village.

Seldom does one find such a traditional village centre as Potten End's village green, which is part of the original Berkhamsted Common. There is the pond with resident and visiting ducks, moorhens, tadpoles and tiddlers to attract the children. Alongside is The Red Lion, one of our two pubs, which draws many visitors to sit outside on a summer's day.

Our other pub, the Plough, looks out on to the Spencer Holland recreation ground, a pleasant green area for the children to play, and beyond this lies the sports field and beautifully attended allotments.

The village still has its own bakery, although the oven is no longer powered by faggots, as it was in the old days when villagers took their Sunday dinners to be cooked. John Groom, whose family has been connected with the bakery since the beginning of the century, is a well-known figure in the village in his smart pony and trap.

Some of the older inhabitants have some interesting tales to tell. One old lady remembers the villagers exercising their common rights by taking out their claims to patches of common, where later they would cut the bracken as bedding for their animals. Another remembered the plaiting school at the bottom of the Front where, in the past, children were taught the craft, and a 96 year old remembers attending as a little girl. A local man walked from Hemel Hempstead each week and on the way he picked up flints which he used to build the walls of the plait school. Part of this wall still stands today.

There are several small industries in the village which give employment locally. Also a garage which helps to keep our wheels turning.

There is a very good bus service to the neighbouring towns which keeps us in touch with wider activities.

Potten End is a caring village and its inhabitants want above all to maintain its traditional atmosphere.

Puckeridge 🖎

Approximately one mile from Standon is the old village of Puckeridge. This was at one time much larger than it is today. It was an important coaching station on the road from London to Cambridge, with 24 coaches passing through and obtaining relays of horses. There were many inns, some of which survive as private houses.

There are three public houses. The Buffalo is situated on the southern fringe and is somewhat isolated from the rest of the village. The Crown and Falcon is about the middle at the junction of High Street and Station Road and the White Hart is found on the Northern fringe. All three are old buildings with the timber frame construction being apparent on the two more central ones. The White Hart is one of the oldest buildings in Puckeridge and at one time the inn's business extended to property across the road.

That much travelled diarist, Samuel Pepys, recorded several incidents at Puckeridge and left us in no doubt that road conditions were far from good. For instance, on 18th September 1661 he wrote: 'The way about Puckeridge very bad, and my wife, in the very last dirty place of all, got a fall, but no hurt, though some dirt. At last she begun, poor wretch, to be tired and I to be angry at it, but I was to blame; for she is a very good companion as long as she is well'.

The state of the roads has improved since Pepys' day, but the way was bad in a different manner until the by-pass was opened for the High Street was the main A10 road, and, as a result was choked with vehicles. Since the traffic was diverted the village has become a quieter, safer place and the people can do their shopping in peace.

Redbourn 🌿

Redbourn is a few miles to the N.W. of St. Albans, its name being derived from 'reedy stream' from the days when reeds grew in abundance along the marshy banks of the river Ver – though still called this, the river now resembles a meandering stream. Redbourn is a large village with 6,000 inhabitants but those who 'Beat the Bounds' have always faced a walk of seventeen miles.

The first known settlement here is the Iron-Age fort 'The Aubrey' to the west. The Romans later built Watling Street, part of which is our High Street of today. The street has brought many travellers over the years. In coaching times there were eighteen inns, now reduced to eight, the Royal Mail coaches changed horses here. Now there is a much campaigned-for bypass, but the High Street remains busy.

Puddingstones are still turned over by the plough in some fields, a large example thought to have been a way-marker now lies near the new bypass in Harpenden Lane whilst another is mounted in the grounds of 'The Priory' in the High Street.

There is a great variation of buildings throughout the village. The Jolly Gardeners, once an inn and now a private dwelling, is the oldest house in the village; farmhouses of note are Wood End Farm and Redbournbury where there is a mill nearby in working order but sadly the water table is now too low for it to function. The Silk Mill is part of a tea and coffee factory, the site of the Jam factory an industrial estate and the Cock Inn a health centre. Cumberland House was once the shooting lodge of the Duke of Cumberland. The Village Hall, once a hat factory is now used regularly for many village events and meetings including productions by Redbourn Players, the weekly W.I. Market, badminton, art exhibitions, dances and the Horticultural Society Shows held in spring and autumn which have been encouraging gardeners to grow bigger marrows since 1883.

138

Dr. Henry Stephens the inventor of Stephens Ink lived at the Bull Inn. St. Amphibalus was reputedly martyred on the Common and Queen Elizabeth I really did sleep here at the Red House when taken ill on a journey from Hatfield House prior to her accession.

Redbourn Common lies to the west of the High Street, is over half a mile long and was presented to the village in 1948 by the Earl of Verulam. It has an avenue of lime trees leading to Church End, where we find the old workhouse with a dutch-gable roof, and the Parish Church which dates from Norman times and which has a beautiful carved rood screen, mentioned in church records in 1479. The screen has rural items carved in the friezes above the panels – a basket of eggs, nuts, grapes and a goose with wing feathers delicately displayed, on either side of the doorway. A number of wild flowers grow on the Common most notably the harebells in August. Flowers of the locality are depicted in an embroidered cloth made and used by the W.I.

The Common is the home of the Cricket Club, the oldest known team in the country, dating from 1666. Matches are played here every week-end during the season with a cricket week in August and the occasional celebrity match. Some of the many lively organisations in the village arrange fetes on the common during the summer, a fair visits twice a year, the village bonfire and fireworks evening is becoming an established event, followed a few days later by the Remembrance Day Service at the War Memorial. There is a tennis club, other sports facilities are being developed with football pitches, the Junior football teams play matches regularly.

Despite the constantly changing population, the proximity of major roads and the ever encroaching development, there still remains a great caring and community spirit in Redbourn. In fact the Redbourn Care Group is well supported and thriving; it is this spirit of care and the friendliness which abounds which endears Redbourn to those who live here.

Roe Green 🐿️

The spelling 'Roe' is found only from the middle 19th century. Before that, the name goes back as 'Rowe' Green to Elizabethan times, and earlier it was 'La Roweth' Green.

Most probably, at the time of the Norman Conquest, the future Roe Green, like most of Hertfordshire in those days, was heavily wooded. Early charters, or the composition of early place names show the presence of oaks, ash trees, hazel and alder.

In the 1851 census there is a complete record of Roe Green. There were 23 houses at the time, and 106 inhabitants, a density of 4.5 persons per house. This meant some overcrowding as many of the cottages had only two bedrooms and a few only one, but the average number of people in one house was not as large as one might expect of Victorian times.

Before the New Town houses were built there were nearly 60 houses in Roe Green, with a further twelve by the New Fiddle in Roe Green Lane which had been built in 1908.

Hatfield became a New Town by the Designation Order of the Minister of Town and Country Planning of 14th June 1948. Roe Green was the first neighbourhood to be designed and built, and work began in 1950, the first house being officially opened on 7th April 1951.

There is no doubt that Roe Green North farm had a much earlier beginning than Roe Green South although this may have been a small croft from about the 16th century. The property was bought by Lord Salisbury (the Prime Minister) and his family continued to own it until it was acquired by the Development Corporation. Mr. A. Hill, who was of Scottish descent, came first as bailiff to Mrs. Vigors early in this century and later became tenant of the farm and was a well known sheep farmer. The earliest owner of Roe Green South farm was Lord Melbourne (of Brocket). It was bought by Lord Salisbury in 1829. Two brothers, named White, were the last tenants and their father first came to Roe Green in 1890. In this century the fields on the east side of Chantry Lane were joined to Roe Green North farm while those on the west remained with Roe Green South. Since the Second World War, Hatfield New Town has been built on the land and the two Roe Green farms have disappeared.

The Old Fiddle public house was first mentioned in 1786, but is probably considerably older than this. It was closed in 1956 and is now a private house. The two cottages standing beside this can be seen on a 1777 map.

The New Fiddle public house (now known as the Cat and Fiddle) is not as new as its name would suggest. It was certainly there in the 1820s and the innkeeper was also the keeper of the toll gate which in those days stood across the entrance to Roe Green Lane.

The Mission Room was the gift of the third Marchioness of Salisbury and was opened in 1888. In the church magazine it said 'a large iron room has been erected. It is hoped it will be appreciated by the inhabitants.' The total seating was over one hundred for a population of not many more than this! In 1953 a sanctuary and vestry were added and the 'tin church' was dedicated in the name of St. John. In 1955 the Cavendish Hall was opened by the Minister of Housing, and a sanctuary at one end of it dedicated by the Bishop of St. Albans and the hall was used instead of the Mission Room for church services. At the same time plans went ahead for a new church at the top of the hill above Roe Green. The foundation stone was laid by Princess Alexandra on 14th June 1958, and St. John's church was completed and consecrated by the Bishop of St. Albans on 26th March 1960.

At the beginning of this century Chantry House was built as one of the earliest sanatoria. Lady Gwendolen Cecil (daughter of the third Marquess of salisbury) was a pioneer in many movements and she decided to prove that tuberculosis could be cured by open-air treatment. Pine trees were planted in the garden and some are still there today, although the building has been demolished, and the houses of Rickfield Close have been built on the land.

Royston

Royston in north-east Hertfordshire nestles at the foot of the Chiltern Hills, right on the Cambridgeshire boundary, with Essex not far away.

The two great roads, around whose crossing Royston grew up, have been highways for possibly 2,000 years. The most ancient, the Icknield Way, first used in Ancient British times, runs west to east from near Falmouth towards Yarmouth, and on the heights running along its length are the ancient barrows, burial places of New Stone Age and Bronze Age man. The other great road, the Ermine Street, running from London to the north, was the great military highway, built by the Romans for their armies. The crossing point of these two great roads was a natural position for a settlement.

By the crossroads was erected, possibly in Saxon times, an ancient stone cross, where travellers would pray for a safe journey. This may have been restored by Lady Rosia, wife of the Lord of

Newsells, William I's steward. She it was, or a relative, who gave Royston its name. The base of the cross, a glacial pebble, remains but the cross has long since vanished.

Nearby in 1184 was founded a small priory, whose many privileges were confirmed by Richard I's charter in 1189. They controlled the weekly market and annual fair, and beneath the shadow of the Priory the community grew. This, like many more, was dissolved by Henry VIII in 1536. Many of the buildings were pulled down, but the spacious chancel of the church was bought by the people of Royston for a Parish Church, which now extended, it still is. There are still to be seen remains of some of the original lancet windows, and the original wooden roof of the south aisle.

Rediscovered in 1742, and also near the Cross is Royston's Cave. Of a circular beehive shape, some 29 feet deep under Melbourn Street, its walls are decorated with an eight foot high frieze of medieval relief carvings, many of a religious character. Its origins are shrouded in mystery, but it is thought to have connections with the Crusaders, possibly the Knights Templar, but nothing can be proved. It is well worth a visit.

Still not far from the Cross, in Kneesworth Street, is the Old Palace. This is the remains of James I's favourite Hunting Lodge, built and used by James I and Charles I on their frequent visits to Royston to enjoy the hunting on the nearby Heath and surrounding hills.

Today, what remains of old Royston is gradually being restored. Look up Upper King Street today. It could be taken straight out of the Middle Ages. The Bull Hotel mentioned in 1520 is still in the High Street, with ancient Tudor houses opposite. The Market Place still has its weekly markets, probably as lively and colourful as centuries ago.

Though steeped in history, Royston is today a flourishing modern community catering for the many and varied needs of its people.

Rushden 🦢

There are probably many stories to tell about the ancient village of Rushden which is in North Hertfordshire. Anthony Trollop visited Julians, the manor and the Duke of Wellington broke his journey at the forge, now known as Old Hammers. The Flemish Ambassador to the court of Queen Elizabeth I owned property here, and legend has it that, so afraid was he of being robbed by outlaws, he buried a ring, a present from the Queen, beneath a walnut sapling in his garden. Inevitably the outlaws attacked and ransacked his house, killing him and throwing his body down a well. The ghastly crime came to light when the Queen sent troops to investigate his prolonged absence from her court. Perhaps the ring lies waiting to be discovered even now.

During the war there were anxious moments when an enemy aircraft unloaded its bombs on its way home to Germany. The craters can still be seen close to the village.

Sadly the village store and post office have closed but we still have our pub, The Moon and Stars which is popular with residents and visitors alike.

St. Ippolyts ﹏

St. Ippolyts (or St. Ippollitts) lies 1½ miles south of Hitchin off the A600. This was the original Welwyn Turnpike road, then only a lane compared with today's standards.

At the crossroads the village store and Post Office is situated on the right with the village hall a few yards further on.

The centre of the main village is approached by the left turn from the main road with directions to the church. At the bottom of the hill on the right is Isaac's iron foundry founded in the middle of the 19th century. As you continue up the hill the Church Parish school faces the T junction. Turn right at the small roundabout and the church dominates the right hand corner. This was originally built in 1087. It was enlarged in the 14th century, and good restoration was carried out in 1840. It is named after Saint Hippolytus the patron saint of horses. Legend has it that services were held where horses were brought to be blessed. This is where the village gets it name and visitors will notice the various ways of spelling seen on the sign posts. The Lych Gate was built in memory of the villagers who gave their lives during the First World War.

There have been many public houses but the more recently known were the Olive Branch and the Jolly Taylors, both now private houses. Nearby is a cottage called The Cottage Loaf, once a bakery and then a grocery store: a recent loss to the community.

Following the road to the left past these and other attractive cottages we come to the new vicarage lying at the end of the now closed road. There are four known sites of the vicarage, the better known of these is St. Ibbs converted from an old coaching inn on the old turnpike road.

The conversion was carried out by the Reverend William Lax about 1800 as the previous vicarage near the school had been burnt down. He straightened the roadway from the front of the house, bought and leased land from Trinity College, Cambridge. He planted trees in the form of his initials W.L. and endeavoured to make the park opposite look like the Backs of Cambridge. To do this he built a bridge (a copy of Trinity College Bridge), dammed the Pirral stream and opened springs to form a lake which has been used for skating. In the winter ice was taken from the lake and stored in the Ice House built underground opposite the lodge. William Lax was a Professor of Astronomy at Cambridge University and he brought with him an observatory said to have been used by Sir Isaac Newton which is still in the garden though now derelict.

A little further on stands the Greyhound and on the outskirts of the village on the road to Welwyn stands the last remaining inn, the Royal Oak.

St. Margarets 🦢

St. Margarets or Stanstead St. Margarets to give it its full name is a very small village divided from Stanstead Abbotts by the river Lee. It is famous for its level crossing which holds up the traffic travelling between the A10 and Harlow. All that will change soon when the Stanstead Abbotts bypass is completed. The cornfield where the gliders landed during the war will soon disappear under the asphalt and there is talk of a new district hospital being built on the bit of field remaining.

Two rivers flow through the parish, the Lee and the New River. Nearby in a field at the southern end of the village there is a shallow depression a few yards long which was the original course of the New River.

We have two pubs and no shops. The Crown used to be called the House up a Tree. There was a treehouse in front of the pub. It was a popular pastime sitting in the branches on a summer evening supping a pint or two. Out at the back is the Crown Hall where we hold our W.I. meetings. It has changed little over the years. I well remember the children's V.E. party in 1945 when we enjoyed paste sandwiches, jelly and blancmange and an enormous Victory cake iced in blue and white, I'd never seen blue icing before. In the evening we had a bonfire party in the field behind the hall with a piano accordian and a singsong. The fire burnt very fiercely and stepping back from the blaze I fell into a large jug of lemonade! I spent the next hour with my back to the fire drying off.

Before the Second World War the main employment in the village was the timber yard. Trees were hauled from all over the county and beyond on large carts pulled by teams of horses, my grandfather was one of the carters. At the yard the trees were sawn into planks and stacked to season. After the war the timber yard was sold and the land used for market gardening which still continues today.

St. Paul's Walden 🌿

St. Paul's Walden acquired its name in 1544 and consists of three villages – St. Paul's Walden, Whitwell and Bendish. However, there had been settlements in the area since the Celts arrived in Hertfordshire between 700 and 500 B.C., and there is evidence of habitation in this parish since then.

Agriculture was and still is the predominant industry in the area, although no longer being the labour-intensive industry it was, the majority of the inhabitants of the parish nowadays work outside the area.

Bendish and St. Paul's Walden are small hamlets on either side of Whitwell and today the whole area is of exceptional interest to people who want to escape into the peace of the countryside, either residentially or for the joys of the country walks. For those with time to spare, a leisurely walk down Whitwell High Street with its fascinating old houses, bears witness to the recent past and the self-sufficiency of the village at the beginning of the century. One could imagine the cattle being driven to the village abattoir; the hustle and bustle at the corn mill and the appetising smells issuing forth from the bakehouse (possibly being offset by those from the tannery and the brewery) where on Sundays parishioners would leave their joints of meat to be cooked whilst they were at church. The noise of the forge would be heard along the High Street and there would be activity around the Straw Plaiting School (straw plaiting for the Luton hat industry was an occupation that village ladies, and children also, carried out to supplement the very low agricultural wages). The buildings housing these local industries still stand to this day, as does the Old Village Hall, a fascinating old building.

The famous Whitwell watercress which at the beginning of the century had a widespread market and was sold in the streets of London for a halfpenny a bunch, continues to be a thriving village industry. The parish also benefits from a local milk service which has been run by the same family for many generations.

All saints, the parish church of St. Paul's Walden, dating back to the 12th century, sits on a hill above Whitwell. One can hear the sound of the Church bells ringing out across the valley on Sunday mornings – a striking contrast to the peace and tranquillity experienced inside the church.

There were three manor houses in the parish at the beginning of the century. The two that still exist are Stagenhoe Park, now a Sue Ryder Home for Physically Handicapped People (and at one time the home of Sir Arthur Sullivan the composer) and St. Paul's Waldenbury. This is the home of the Bowes Lyon family and is where the Queen Mother spent part of her childhood years. On certain Sundays in the summer, the gardens of St. Paul's Waldenbury are open to the public and provide the opportunity for relaxation in lovely surroundings.

Whitwell has at some time been the home of Sir Francis Camps, the forensic pathologist and also Alan Sillitoe the novelist and Robert Newton the actor lived here.

Sandon 🐝

Early man decided to settle at Sandon because of the plentiful supply of water to be found there. Numerous small ponds were formed in depressions in the boulder clay high up on the Chiltern hills. Such villages are called 'Pond Villages'.

When the Domesday Book was compiled in 1086, Sandon was listed as having one priest with 24 villagers, and a total value of £16. It now consists of over 4,000 acres, and a much increased population.

Most of the parish is above the 400 ft. contour line, with the highest point just behind the church, which looks down on fields, and a well-scattered community.

There is little doubt that from earliest times the site at present occupied by the Church of All Saints has been used for worship of some kind. It was originally a timber building with daub and wattle walls, but before the 10th century it was altered to a dark barn-like building. It was converted to its present form in 1348. The tower contains five bells. The treble is undated, the second is marked 1721, the third 1728, the fourth 1709, and the tenor bell 1624. Across the road from the church stands a public house called The Six Bells where many ringers must have quenched their thirsts after pulling the other five!

In olden times, May Day was the great spring festival, and in Sandon the young men went a-maying just after midnight, leaving bunches of hawthorn at the doors of the larger houses while singing the Mayer's Song. Later the same morning they called again at each house for 'largess' (a present, or reward) dressed in white smocks decorated with ribbons, and wearing tall silk hats with bightly-coloured ribbons and streamers hanging down their backs. They carried a basket, and in the evening 'made feast' with what they had collected.

Another time for feasting according to the old English almanacs was 1st August. called 'Lammas Day'. The name means Loaf-Mass, or Bread-Mass, signifying a thanksgiving for the first gathering of corn. This was often called 'Lammas Wheat' and bread was baked with it for the feast. Many Hertfordshire parishes had commons called Lammas Lands, and in Sandon there is still a Lammas Meadow.

In recent times, Sandon has become known for the annual two-day Flower Festival which is held each September. Visitors come from afar to see the magnificent floral arrangements in the Church – some from London hiring a coach each year to bring them. A dedicated team of skilful ladies in the village think and plan for months, as each year the beautiful arrangements depict a different theme. Even the children take part, for in the vestry samples of their art are displayed with pictures from the Bible lovingly por-trayed in bright colours. Arts and crafts made by the local inhabi-tants are on view in the nearby school, while in the village hall, home-made meals and light refreshments soon disappear. On the Sunday evening a special Flower Festival Evensong is held, the church tower is then floodlit, and can be seen across the fields for miles.

During the Second World War, Sandon had its share of action. Over 70 bombs, a few incendiaries, and a rocket fell within its boundaries. One incident could have had disastrous consequences when a bomb landed on the road without exploding. Several of the villagers had gone to see where it had landed, and peered down into the hole. Later, just after a car had gone by, the bomb went off. Fortunately, no-one was injured.

Friendly people who willingly give help in times of need create the happy atmosphere that is found here. They have raised thousands of pounds for various charities, and it is these kindly inhabitants who make Sandon a very charming village in which to live.

Sandridge 🦢

Sandridge village lies approximately three miles north-east of the Cathedral city of St. Albans on what was the Roman road from St. Albans to Royston – part of which is now the B561. It was quite an established village at the time of the Domesday Book and, according to historians, there is evidence that some kind of settlement existed as far back as 54 B.C.

In Saxon times it was known as Sandruage, so called due to the sandy soil and 'age' signified the service of the bond tenants. It is pronounced 'Sarndridge' by the locals.

Although Sandridge was decimated by the Black Death and two battles were fought on nearby Nomansland common in the Middle Ages, its existence continued, no doubt due to the influence of well known 'gentry' such as the Jennings family. Sarah Jennings married John Churchill (later Duke of Marlborough) who took the title of Lord churchill of Sandridge in her honour when he was made a peer. One of the daughters of that marriage married Charles Spencer and their off-spring, John, became the first Earl Spencer. To this day the Earl Spencer is the 'patron of the living and nominal Lord of the Manor', even though he resides at Althorp in Northamptonshire.

Sandridgebury situated half a mile from the village centre is the largest house, being built during the reign of Queen Anne and is now a listed building. Always a private dwelling until recently when it became a school for a few years. It has now been restored and divided into three dwellings in one of which a member of the Thrale family lives. This family has had strong historical ties with the village since the early 1500s.

There are a number of large farms within the parish surrounding the village. In the late 1920s the Salvation Army bought two adjoining farms, which they continue to farm, one being known as Pound Farm, a 350 year old farmhouse situated beside the High Street. This farm used to be fronted by six mighty elms reputed to have been planted by Sarah Jennings but now sadly only four ivy covered half trunk shells remain. The Salvation Army also have a home for the elderly, Lyndon. This is the former vicarage in the village next to the church. They also have several flats and houses for their retired officers. The lower end of the High Street used to become flooded during the rising of the springs and so the village acquired its nickname 'Sandridge Docks'.

It was always a very poor village with a workhouse to accommodate the poor and needy families. This was demolished and replaced by council houses. It can now happily be classified as a village with very few poor inhabitants.

Since the Second World War quite a lot of council and private development has taken place, not greatly altering the long High Street which gives the impression of ribbon development – a continuation of St. Albans. Due to the close proximity of that city and to a reasonably efficient bus service the shopping facilities within the village have almost ceased to exist. Only one small general/newsagent store, an off licence and Post Office (the latter had to be fought for to be retained) and three public houses, two of which go back to being coaching inns. The village store was in the late 1800s and early 1900s the bakery to which villagers took their Sunday joints to be cooked for a small charge.

The village is still very rural in its surroundings and it is hoped it will manage to retain its farmlands, woods, lanes and footpaths for many years to come and to maintain a village way of life.

Sarratt 🦋

'A long and wide village green and houses standing alongside its edge'. The historian who described Sarratt thus would probably not have any difficulty in recognising our village today. True he would not find the saddlery, forges, wheelwrights, shops or indeed the two bakehouses, all long since gone. But the dell, old pump and pond are still part of the Sarratt scene today, together with the flint cottages and two inns.

In the 10th century the spelling of the name was Syret and from the 11th to 13th centuries it was Syreth and after three other versions became Sarrett in the 16th century and finally to Sarratt in the 17th century. We did not rate a mention in the Domesday Book which infers that the land did not produce any profit for the King. As the St. Albans Times of 1862 neatly puts it 'thou wast past o'er in Domesday Times and ministered not to the Conqueror's needs'.

It is believed that Sarratt probably lay on a drovers' route, the green with its three ponds being an ideal stopping place. Not only would the sheep be sure of grass and water but the drovers could also refresh themselves in one of the inns which surrounded the green. In living memory there were five inns overlooking the green, now reduced to two, the oldest of which is The Boot which bears the date 1739 (reputed to have changed hands in the 17th century for £1).

In 1859 Edward Ryley became Rector of Sarratt Parish Church, and to him the village is indebted for the scrap book he compiled using cuttings from newspapers, posters and photographs – anything of interest connected with Sarratt. After he died, subsequent Rectors have carried on adding to the scrap book up to present times which has given us a fascinating insight into our village life over the past 120 years.

The Green, the heart of the village, has been the scene of many celebrations for royal occasions. Both the festivities for the 1897 Diamond Jubilee and Queen Victoria's 80th birthday in 1899 included children's sports, fancy dress parades, sumptuous teas, bonfires and fireworks. The story goes that during the 1899 celebrations an effigy of Kruger with gunpowder in his hat was ceremoniously burned. Torches were lit and Mr. Simmonds with his American Organ on a van played music for the occasion. Many other royal celebrations have taken place up to present times. The Jubilee in 1935 and the Coronations of 1937 and 1953 were marked by planting oak trees on the Green where they stand tall and proud today.

It must have come as a great relief when in the early 1920s a water supply was laid onto the village. Previously water had to be drawn from the village well, described as looking like a huge knife cleaning machine. It took rigorous pumping to get the mechanism working in the morning so nobody was eager to be the first to draw water. In 1975, Architectural Year, some of the money allocated to Sarratt was used to provide a new casing for the pump.

Sarratt got lit-up in 1932 when electricity arrived. The switching-on ceremony was carried out by the Chairman of the Parish Council and there followed a two-day exhibition showing the latest appliances and uses to which the current could be put.

Another annual attraction is the May Day Fair whose origins are lost in antiquity. It is believed it was started by Royal Charter and the continuity must not be broken otherwise the right to bring the fair to Sarratt will be lost. During the Second World War just one caravan and either a children's round-about or swinging boats would arrive thus giving credence to the story. The fair is now so large that hardly a blade of grass on the Green is visible and for two days the village reverberates with music and noise.

In 1982 the village reached new heights when it won the Best Kept Village competition and proudly displayed the handsome sign for a year. And Sarratt today? A mixture of cottages, old and new houses, modern bungalows, council houses and flats, all blending in quite happily which can also be said of the villagers, the W.I. having played an important role over the past 30 years in providing the opportunity to meet and mix. Fourth and even fifth generation Sarrattonians have accepted the 'incomers' who have chosen to move and settle into this delightful Hertfordshire Village.

Sawbridgeworth 🦚

In the extreme east of the county, on the banks of the river Stort, lies Sawbridgeworth, a delightful blend of past and present set in the belt of woods and fields between Bishop's Stortford and Harlow.

From archaeological finds we know there has been a settlement on this site for many thousands of years.

In the Domesday Book Sabrixteworde is recorded as having a church dedicated to St. Mary with a priest-in-charge. There were about 200 inhabitants one of whom owned a mill. At that time the village formed part of the estate of Geoffrey de Mandeville, whose name lives on in the 120 pupil Mandeville Primary School.

In 1306 a charter was granted for a market and fair to be held in Sawbridgeworth. The fair is still held each year in April and October, but is now just a small funfair. There are still local residents who can remember the time when the fair was one of the notable dates in the village calendar. The first day of the April fair was a horse show, and buying and selling of horses went on all day. At the end of the last century the village children, who had a holiday from school for the fair, were able to spend their farthings on bags of treacle toffee or sherbert with liquorice straws, all made by Mrs. Cockton, a local resident. The fair occupied all the Market Square and Fair Green, and today there is still a charming green, a village pump, fine old houses and quaint shops in this area.

In the market square an early 16th century building still stands, with its timber-framed walls and the distinctive feature of an overhang across the hall range, which is extremely rare. It is now the Market House Hotel, displaying its many fine features to all its patrons.

Down Church Street is the gateway to the 600 year old Great St. Mary's church, which has one of the finest collections of monumental sculpture in the country. Today visitors from many countries come to take brass rubbings in this beautiful church.

Well-known in horticultural circles was the fruit nursery founded in Sawbridgeworth by John Rivers in 1725, and claimed to be one of the first of its kind in the country. Several varieties of fruit trees developed here still carry the 'Rivers' name. Peach trees were first planted here about the time of Nelson's victory at Trafalgar. Many of their fruit trees are still to be found in the gardens of modern houses which now occupy the land which the Rivers family cultivated for over 250 years.

Shenley 🍂

Shenley lies south of St. Albans in the Green Belt and thankfully has not been completely overwhelmed by the London sprawl. Sitting high on a spur of the Chilterns, we are told that it is as high as the cross on top of St. Pauls Cathedral in London.

Shenley appears in the Domesday Book of 1086 under the old spelling of Scenlai and, in an old charter, which is preserved in the British Museum, it was given to the Abbots of St. Albans Monastery before the reign of King Harold.

The area round Shenley became popular with the aristocracy and gentry anxious to leave London smells and sickness. Large estates dotted the landscape and they were our first commuters, as London was only an easy ride away.

Nell Gwynne lived at moated Salisbury Hall, which during the Second World War was taken over by De Havillands and the first prototype of the Mosquito was built there. As the village is on the old pilgrims' route from London to St. Albans, King Henry VIII and Queen Katherine of Aragon passed through on their way to stay at Tyttenhanger.

Nicholas Hawksmoor the famous architect lies buried in the churchyard of St. Botolphs, which was the original parish church. He was a pupil of Christopher Wren and helped to design St. Paul's Cathedral. He designed churches in the city of London, Oxford and Cambridge, also collaborated with Vanburgh in the design of Blenheim Palace. Hawksmoor lived at Porters Park, a very attractive mansion with lovely grounds, which also had Admiral Earl Howe, a contemporary of Lord Nelson, as an occupier. Much later in 1934 this estate became Shenley Hospital and during the war years it became a military hospital.

There are four inns in the village within hailing distance of each other. Sadly several of the shops have disappeared, but the school for the 5 to 9 year olds remains.

There are many reminders of the old Shenley still around, the old village lock-up called The Cage stands by the pond. Law breakers were put in there overnight before being taken by horse and cart to Barnet to appear before the Bench. The inscriptions over the two small barred windows state, 'Do well and fear naught', and 'Be sober, be vigilant', advice still to be heeded. The pond is quite a feature and years ago geese and ducks belonging to nearby villagers enjoyed the scene. Not far away from the pond is the Village Hall, part of which was the original girls school. The club house next door where the caretaker now lives was built to meet the needs of single men who were working in the area. Also there was a reading room and classes were held there. Pound Lane and Pound House are reminders of the old Pound near the Black Lion where straying animals were kept. Luckily many of the old cottages and houses are still intact and these help to maintain the rural nature of the village.

Spitalbrook 🪶

The area known as Spital is on the boundary which used to exist between the estates of Hoddesdonbury and Baas Manors. It later marked the offical border line between the then small residential area of Broxbourne and the larger one of Hoddesdon itself when Hoddesdon had an Urban District Council.

The traveller from London many years ago had to pass through a toll gate at the upper part of Spitalbrook Hill to enter Spital. At the base of the hill there was a group of cottages built by a Mr. John Warner and later the residential suburb of St. Catherines was built by the two brothers Hunt. There was also an ancient hospital on the corner which in 1642 came to be used as a tavern.

The brook which runs under the road now and is mainly piped is known as Spitalbrook and flows almost unnoticed. There was a bridge over the brook in 1835 with wooden rails on each side and no brick parapet. Before this bridge was built there were fords at Woollensbrook and Spitalbrook.

The water flowing into the brook, according to notes from a former employee of the water board early this century, comes via Woolensbrook from a spring at Hertford Heath. He commented that the spring probably comes via the chalk of Dunstable Downs, eventually flows into the river Lea and thence to the sea.

Apparently Broxbourne maintenance engineers were often in trouble with judges for not maintaining the portion of the High Road which suffered from water running from the high ground to the west of Spitalbrook. There used to be two drinking troughs supplied by pipe from this water, one at the top of the hill opposite the entrance to what is now St. Michaels Road and one at the entrance to St. Davids Drive, at the bottom of the hill.

All is very different now but the water still flows under the road and can still be seen as a little brook in the garden of a house near the George Inn and similarly a house at the corner of St. Catherines Road.

Standon 🐚

Although the parish of Standon is large, the village itself is basically one wide street which narrows as it curves sharply just past the church. Its open aspect is due to the fact that it was once a market town that rivalled that of Ware. A number of the buildings are of old or ancient timber frame construction, concealed in several by a cladding of brick added later. Their different styles blend harmoniously to produce a delightful picture.

There are two public houses, the Bell and the Star, both housed in 17th-century timber framed buildings.

The church is dedicated to St. Mary, and was built by the Knights Hospitaller of St. John of Jerusalem. Standing next to it is the brick and timber building that was the local school until the new one was opened in Station Road in 1974. It has been considered for many years that this building was once the Hospice of the Knights of St. John, known to have existed during their occupation of the manor, but the suggestion has recently been made that the Post Office building was that Hospice and that the old school was originally a Guildhall. It is of a somewhat later date than would be expected of a building erected by the Knights.

The almshouses adjoining the old school were originally weavers' sheds and had a thatched roof until 1964 or 65 which accounts for the very high chimney stacks.

On a green opposite the old school stands a large piece of Hertfordshire puddingstone on a flint base. This used to be at the church gate, where it was used as a mounting block.

The lane beyond leads to the river Rib, on the banks of which is Paper Mill House. This was formerly a water mill making the very fine paper on which bibles were printed. The water wheel was *in situ* until six or seven years ago.

Standon was in the hands of the Abbot of Croyland in Lincolnshire up to the time of the Norman Conquest, but William granted it to William Gifford, whose daughter was in possession when the Domesday Book was compiled in 1086. It was her son, Gilbert de Clare, who made the bequest of 140 acres of land, a vineyard and the Church of Standon to the Knights Hospitaller of St. John of Jerusalem. The Order held the property for nearly 400 years until dispossessed by Henry VIII when he disbanded the Order. The Knights are credited with the building of the church. It is possible that they used the site of the Abbot of Croyland's earlier chapel. It is known that the present chancel was built about 1230 on to the nave of an older church and that the nave itself was re-built about 1345, with the West porch and the tower being added in the 15th century. Until it was necessary to construct the organ chamber the tower was an independent building separated from the church by a grassed area bounded only by two low walls.

On the south side of the altar is the imposing memorial, with its marble effigy of Sir Ralph Sadleir, Standon's most illustrious inhabitant. He was an important statesman in the service of both Henry VIII and Elizabeth I. Mounted near his monument are the staff of the banner he captured at the battle of Pinkie during Henry's war with Scotland. Also there are his spurs, halberd and helmets. Sir Ralph was the ambassador sent by Henry to see Mary, Queen of Scots, as a three month old baby, to find out if she would make a suitable wife for Prince Edward. Many years later, when already an old man, he was appointed custodian of the Scottish Queen. He obtained release from this charge and retired to Standon where he died 30th March 1587, seven weeks after Mary was beheaded.

Standon has had its share of eccentric inhabitants. There was the gravedigger and sexton, Daniel Clerk, who would dig up old bones to make room for the newly dead. He kept a large basket of old bones in his cottage and claimed to know whose remains they were. It is thought he was the prototype of Charles Dickens' gravedigger.

There was also Richard Gaff, born 1706, who, at the age of 95 married his fifth wife aged 29. She gave him five children in 16 years: one born before marriage in 1800. He died in 1819, aged 113 years!

Stanstead Abbotts ❧

A large village of some 2,000 inhabitants at the northern end of the Lea Valley Park, contributing an extensive Yachting Marina and many walks to that project.

Well provided with shops, it serves several surrounding villages, and has a wide variety of small businesses, many located in ex-malting buildings which once were the centre of our chief source of employment.

Probably best known for its level crossing and congested High Street, its natives look forward to the completion of a bypass by 1987, which should return the village to something near its pre-war peacefulness.

Two of the oldest buildings in the village stand opposite one another at the notorious Pied Bull corner – the Clockhouse, once a Dame School, and the Red Lion. Another old village landmark, the Countess of Huntingdon's Chapel has been disused for three years.

The old School in Roydon Road was built in 1869 with the same architect (Waterhouse) as St. Pancras Station and Easneye. The latter, now occupied by All Nations College for Missionary Students, stands high on the northern edge of the village in about 130 acres of magnificent parkland.

The excellent train service to London makes Stanstead Abbotts a commuters' haven and many houses have been erected in recent years; the latest estate, now under construction, being on the railway's ex-goods yard.

Also within the parish, though two miles from the village, is Rye House Castle where a plot to assassinate Charles II was hatched. All that remains is the Gate House and a shallow moat. In contrast there is a modern go-carting track just opposite and a large sewage farm serving Stevenage not far away, beside what was once a toll road with its large board listing charges for carts and animals, now still a toll road but only for motor vehicles.

Briggens, once the home of Lord Aldenham, is now a large and up-to-date country hotel with a 9-hole golf course, while Nether-field House, once occupied by Booths (of gin fame) now, by coincidence, is a Salvation Army Home for elderly gentlemen.

The river Lea, which forms our western boundary, is no longer used by barges to and from London, but is much used by long boats from Ware and by fishermen from all quarters, while the lakes left from recent gravel excavations have made a huge habitat for wild birds, of great interest to birdwatchers.

The Parish Council of nine works hard on behalf of the village keeping an eye on housing, churchyards, car parking and traffic problems etc., while the Ashlea Amenity Society also monitors these items, encourages householders with annual prizes for best kept gardens and each spring plants bulbs etc. along our roadsides.

Altogether, a busy and growing community with something for everyone to join in.

Tewin 🌿

Formerly confined to Upper Green and Lower Green, the village now encompasses to the north a settlement begun in the inter-war period in Punchetts Wood (the Punchehed coppyes of 1544) and known now as Tewin Wood, a rare example of 'arcadia in its purest form – an individualistic estate of wealthy houses, developed in a woodland setting'.

Many of the cottages which stood at Upper Green have gone, but the 17th-century Plume of Feathers remains, possibly on the site of one alehouse 'allowed' to Tewin by the County Justices in 1596. Upper Green is today the scene of tennis and football, and especially cricket matches, which are famous for being reported occasionally in *The Times* by one of the team players, Simon Barnes, continuing the tradition of Tewin as a great centre for the game in the 18th and 19th centuries. Matches were then played at all seasons, with a joint of meat or a free meal for the winners; a crowd of 1,500 is recorded as watching a game here in the early 1800s between Tewin and Ware, followed by supper (for the players only, one assumes) down the road at the Rose and Crown.

Along this road, near Tewin garage is the turning to Tewin Hill. Beyond it lies the mullioned mansion of Queen Hoo Hall. Known in 1060 as Quenildehaga, 'enclosure of a woman named Cwēnhild', the present house, through whose courtyard is supposed to have passed Queen Elizabeth I, was built about 1550, and its name was the title of an unfinished romantic novel, set in Tewin, by the antiquary and engraver Joseph Strutt. He died, leaving it to be completed by Sir Walter Scott, and published in 1808.

Queen Hoo stands about 30m above Lower Green, on which most of the modern village has grown, with extensive development since the Second World War. Tewin's strategic location in proximity to business and industry in Welwyn Garden City, within three miles of the A1(M) to the west and five minutes drive of fast mainline services to London and a short distance from the M25 makes it a prime residential area. Much of its attraction lies in its essentially rural character which is closely guarded by the local amenity society and so far preserved by the Green Belt regulations which proscribe any further extension of the village.

The green itself was reconstructed early in 1953 in preparation for the coronation celebrations; the area was ploughed and resown, a Y-shaped concrete path was made, the grass seed being donated by Major Lines, who also gave a 'pig and a bottle of whisky' to raise funds. In that year, the roofed cover to the old well (by then gone) was moved across to form a bus shelter, which then faced the dilapidated old forge, now pulled down but commemorated in the name of a near-by cottage. Gone too from the green are the old stocks, remembered by Cecil Deades as there in his boyhood in the 1850s. The school finally moved from its village green site in 1974, but left behind an attractive early victorian (1838) building, now converted into two private homes; facing the school across the green is the Old School House, probably of early 18th-century origin, where in 1773 was begun a school for 10 poor children, funded by Henry Yarborough.

The Beit family lived in Tewin Water, a mile away. Originally a 17th-century house, it was rebuilt in its present imposing form in 1798, with extensive grounds landscaped by Repton. Born in Hamburg, the Beit brothers became renowned diamond magnates and friends of Cecil Rhodes. They gave millions to deserving causes and were finally buried in Tewin churchyard. Lady Beit left Tewin Water in 1946 and it was sold in 1951 for £14,750 to Hertford-shire County Council who converted it to a school for deaf children.

A former incumbent of Tewin Water, and to whom a tablet stands in the church, was Lady Cathcart. Three times widowed, she had inscribed on her next wedding ring 'If I survive, I will have five'; but her fourth husband, who was seventeen years her junior, imprisoned her in Ireland, spending her money, until his death twenty years later. She returned to Tewin to recover her property and lived to be 98, but did not venture again into matrimony.

Her story is told in Maria Edgeworth's novel, *Castle Rackrent* (1800). This account gives her former abode as Tewin House, where lived for twenty-four years her second husband's cousin, General Joseph Sabine. He died in 1739, having distinguished himself in Marlborough's campaigns; a large monument to his name is to be found inside the church porch. His home, Tewin House was reputedly the most elegantly furnished house in the county when it was pulled down in 1807 by its last owner, Peter, fifth Earl Cowper. There is now only a garden wall and uneven ground to mark its former presence.

On the other side of this wall lies the church, remarkable for its 11th, 13th and 15th century architecture. Here are to be found more graves of the area's past eminents: the Botelers and de Havillands (of aeronautical fame) and in particular, that of Lady Anne Grimston of Gorehambury who died in 1733 and around whom was woven in Victorian times a libellous legend, declaiming her an unbeliever in the Resurrection and who is supposed to have said 'If indeed there is life after death, trees will render asunder my tomb'. Several trees have grown out of her tomb, and in spite of strong denials of her faithlessness by the Earl of Verulam, by 1874, thousands were visiting the grave annually, wearing away wide paths in the turf. She is still held in awe by the church bellringers, who for countless years have, on the stroke of midnight when ringing out the passing of the old year, left the belfry tower, raced out and around Lady Grimston's tomb, to return before the final stroke of twelve, lest they should be haunted by her ghost.

Therfield 🌿

The village of Therfield which stands on the ridge of the Chilterns is very old. On Therfield Heath there are long barrows which would indicate that the area was inhabited in the iron age. Indeed this would not be surprising since the position of the village overlooking the Icknield Way, now in that part of the A505, would make it a natural place for habitation.

The Anglo-Saxon translation of the village name is 'dry land' and in the Domesday Book the entries record that 'the value is 10 shillings and before 1066, twenty shillings' further 'that Aelfric, a priest, held this land under the Abbott of Ramsey and that he could not sell without the Abbot's permission'. The Abbots remained Lords of the Manor of Therfield until the Dissolution of the Monasteries in the reign of Henry VIII and it then passed into the hands of the King who in 1541 presented it to his new Queen Katherine Howard. Subsequently it was passed to the Dean and Chapter of St. Paul's in London. The old village church was probably built in the 13th century but this, because of subsidence was demolished in 1874 and the new church which was built was much larger than its predecessor. At that time it had no tower, so the call to church was made by a single bell hung in a tree.

Throughout the centuries Therfield has always been, and for that matter, still is an agriculturally based village. At one time it was far larger than it is at present. It is recorded that in 1856 there were 325 children under 14 years of age but because of rural depopulation by 1934 the number of children attending the village school had fallen to 68 and this included some from the neighbouring village of Kelshall.

On a less sober note there were seven public houses and in addition two off-licences. Now there are none of the latter and only two public houses namely, the Fox and Duck on the village green and the Bell on the road between Therfield and Kelshall.

However, for all of the reduction in population Therfield has kept very much abreast of the times. In the past it has won the much sought after title of Best Kept Village in Hertfordshire organised by the Hertfordshire Society, for small villages, six times, due to a community effort by everyone living in the village keeping and maintaining their own area.

While the occupations of the villagers have changed from agriculture to Commerce and Industry it has not become a commuter village but one where the interests of the community are very much to the forefront.

Thorley

The Manor of Thorley was held by Godid in the reign of Edward the Confessor. After the Norman Conquest, however, when William of Normandy ruled the country, he sold or gave parts of the land to his nobles and Bishops and by 1086 the manorial rites of Thorley had been acquired by Geoffrey de Magnaville one of William's gallant followers (hence the road named Magnaville on our new estate). It was said to be given to him for the part he played in the overthrow of Harold at the battle of Hastings.

It was while Geoffrey de Magnaville was Lord of the Manor that the Domesday Book was completed. In this book Thorley is called Torlei; Tor meaning Rocky Hill and Lei meaning meadow or pasture, and we find Thorley had 28 houses, 80 men, women and children, a mill, pasture for cattle, woodland for 40 hogs, a priest and a knight.

Then in the reign of Henry III the manor was held by Richard de Thorley who probably took his name from the place, and it was during this 13th century that the Nave and Chancel of the church were built in the early English style, but no doubt on the site of an earlier Norman Church. The first known rector was instituted on

13th April 1327 in the reign of Edward III. The tower was built later in the 15th century in the Perpendicular style.

In the reign of Henry IV the manor seems to have been divided for a time. Sir Richard Whittington who was 3 times Lord Mayor of London was also the famous Dick Whittington of cat and bells fame, and believed to be the Lord of the Manor from 1399 to 1413. Hence the name of Richard Whittington School and Whittington Way.

Another person who owned part of the manor in the reign of Henry V was John Pynchbek. In the same reign the manor passed into the possession of John Leventhorpe and remained in the Leventhorpe family until the reign of Charles II in 1672, a total of 250 years.

During this time Thorley had a very famous Rector Francis Burley one of the revisers of the Authorised Bible in 1611.

The acreage of the original parish was 1,527 acres of land and 9 of water. During this period various farms were developed. Mentioned in the Close Rolls of 1397 is one named Nicolas Rumbard who probably farmed Rumbalds Farm. In the Court Rolls 1417 a Richard Boteler was no doubt associated with Butlers Hall. Then later on Castle Farm is mentioned in Court Rolls 1603 to 1625, Stone Hall as Stone Hill, Thorley Hall and Thorley Street are also mentioned. Moor Hall is shown as More Hall in the letters of Henry VIII. Henry VIII gave it to Sir Henry Parker the eighth Baron Morely. He was a gentleman usher to Henry VIII and his daughter married Anne Boleyn's brother. It is said that the man who warned Parliament about the Gunpowder plot rode to London from Moor Hall. We know that it was to a grandson of Lord de Morely of Hallingbury Place that the letter warning him not to attend Parliament was delivered.

Thundridge

Much of the land around Thundridge was owned by the Hanbury family, who were brewers. The family house was Poles Mansion, which for some years now has been a convent school, but is to close shortly and has been sold to developers. Many of the woods in the area still show signs of ancient coppicing, the timber having been used in the nearby maltings in Ware.

A lovely sign gives an easily recognisable name to the Public House in Thunderidge, 'The Sow and Pigs', which contains a vast collection of Travellers Cards. The name is believed to have derived from an 18th-century card game said to have been popular with farmers called 'My Sow's Pigg'd'. It had formerly been called the Five Horseshoes and The Fox.

Passing Thundridge Church, St. Marys, high on the hillside the stranger may not realise that the ruins of a much older Place of Worship lie to the east of the village along the lane to the nearby hamlet of Cold Christmas. The four bells in the new church, the angels round the tower and the heads of a medieval king and queen in the church came from the old church. Only the roofless tower of the old one remains.

Down the hill passing Thundridge village school, and a section of the old Ermine Street flanked by some pretty 18th-century cottages, and the Windmill Public House we come into Wadesmill, where the main road passes over the River Rib. Where the old water mill stood a replica has been recently built and is a private dwelling. It is reputed that Thomas-a-Becket, who lived in the area, fell into the River Rib at this point, and the miller stopped his work and jumped into the water and saved him.

Just over the bridge is the large Feathers Inn, once one of the main coaching stops between London and Cambridge. When it was first built in 1615 it was known as The Prince's Arms and had stabling for one hundred horses. It is now a pleasant carvery, and is said to be haunted by the ghost of a young girl who was run over by a coach. The village fair used to be held in the meadow behind the inn on 16th June each year, but now only the village fete remains.

Opposite is the Anchor Inn, popular with locals. It boasts of home made Cornish Pasties made by the landlady Mrs. Lucy Locket, from Plymouth.

To the East of Wadesmill is Youngs Manor, or Youngsbury, as it is now known. A Roman settlement was discovered in the grounds, including an underground ice house and pottery. The latter is now in St. Albans Museum. The present house was built in about 1700, with some later additions. The parkland was laid out by Capability Brown. In 1857 the estate passed to Christopher William Puller, who had licence to add the name Giles before his surname. The family name has left many marks on the area to this day.

Totteridge ✌

A long village with the main part built on a ridge. There is a Green and a Common, where as recently as 1945, the commoners still had grazing rights. Totteridge was first mentioned in 1219 A.D. when the Bishop of Ely was Lord of the Manor. The last person to hold that office died in 1938, and after the end of the 1939-1945 War, a Manor Association was formed by the residents to protect the region from urban development.

Many well-signposted footpaths run through the district, passing along unspoilt countryside. The Darlands Nature Reserve consists of lake, marsh and woodland. It is along the flight path of migratory birds, and has interesting flora and fauna.

It is known that a chapel existed here in 1250. The present church of St. Andrew was built here in 1799; this is on the site of at least two earlier buildings. The yew tree in the churchyard is over 900 years old. Beside the church is the village pound of 1560, and a 17th-century tithe barn. Nearby on a small green, stands the War Memorial. The Cedar was planted to commemorate the end of the Crimea War in 1856.

There are many fine houses in the district. On the corner of Barnet Lane (which was a road in 1360) stands The Priory built around 1500, where a priests hole has been discovered. Also in this Tudor house is an open hearth, with an iron fireback 'Carolius Rex 1640'. In the front of the building are two oriel windows, at the rear are unspoilt 16th century bricks and chimneys. In recent years Yehudi Menuhin was a frequent visitor, when the musician Archibald Camden lived there.

Opposite the church stands Garden Hill, an early Georgian house, and Southernhay of the Queen Anne period. From here there are delightful views across the Totteridge valley. In the centre of the village are several 18th century cottages, and a small nonconformist chapel, now a private dwelling. Walking along the lane towards Mill Hill is the Manor House built in 1691, and Totteridge Park, a fine red brick building, built for the Duke of Chandos in 1748, under which there is a 14th century undercroft, no doubt part of a monastery or chapel. Willow House was originally a Tudor farmhouse, and named Denham. Further along the lane is West End House, a Queen Anne building with a barn of the same date. Nearly opposite this house is Fairlawn, the original part was built in 1710. Hitler's ambassador, Ribbentrop stayed here just before the outbreak of war in 1939.

We still have our village school on the common, and pub, The Orange Tree, but not a shop – that closed down a few years ago. The whole of the original Totteridge is in a Conservation Area, and is surrounded by Green Belt Land.

Tring 🍂

There is much written evidence to prove that Tring (or something very like that name) was here 1,000 years ago and there have been fascinating finds indicating human habitation from much earlier times. Two ancient highways, still in use today, the Icknield Way and Akeman Street contributed to Tring's importance as a market town. Holloways, through which cattle were herded and peasants walked, have revealed much of interest to the expert and scholar.

At one time Tring was a home to the Dissenters and we have elegant Baptist chapels and a Quaker graveyard still today. We claim a connection with the United States in so far as the great grandfather of President George Washington hailed from here.

Lord Rothschild of Tring was a generous benefactor and we have open spaces, a meeting Hall, a hospital (now a clinic), many solid Victorian buildings and countless small houses built for their employees which continue to charm the newcomer.

Tring Show, still an eagerly awaited annual event, was the highspot of the year. Some 20,000 people came from near and far and entered into the spirit of the day. There were flower shows, agricultural competitions, sheepdog trials, milling and poultry shows, horsejumping and to crown it all a firework display to enrapture the throng. Where we now have a fish and chip shop and a Chinese takeaway were small shops selling cherry pies at the end of the day!

Lord Rothschild's elder son Walter was encouraged in an ever-developing interest in animals. Emu and wallaby are remembered roaming in the grounds and at one stage zebras were harnessed to draw a cart. Walter Rothschild's collection formed the basis of what is now Tring museum attracting as it does many thousands of children with their parents together with a more serious re-search side, was a unique gift to the nation and to Tring.

When the Rothschilds left the Mansion Tring began to change. Family shops, at one time all the way up and down each side of the High Street, closed and were eventually replaced today by estate agents. Corner shops, in the main, disappeared forever. Inns and pubs, once alert to the visits of royalty to the mansions, lost their sparkle, and in some cases closed. In more recent days Tring has welcomed many Londoners to its midst and it is getting even more difficult to 'see the join'.

Serious walkers all know Tring and canal buffs have a great time. Our reservoirs are now Nature Reserves and internationally known for their wildfowl visitors. Tring has changed and of course will continue to do so – let us hope some of it will be for the better.

Walkern 🌿

According to legend, in the Middle Ages when Boxbury was a village its people began to build a church but each night their carefully laid stones were reassembled on a site by the river Beane. It was, of course, the work of the devil, who was heard to encourage the movement of the building materials with the cry 'Walk on'! 'Walk on'! But, this being Hertfordshire, what he said was 'Walkern'. Thus, when the village thought it prudent to adopt the devil's choice of site the new settlement already had a name.

The devil had not finished with Walkern, if the trial in 1711 of Jane Wenham – the last person to be condemned to death for witchcraft in England – is any evidence. Jane lived in a hovel, now long vanished, in Church Lane. Accused among other things of bewitching sheep and farm labourers, she was sent for trial in Hertford and sentenced to death. However, granted the Queen's pardon, too terrified to return to her home, she went to Hertingfordbury where she lived for the rest of her life.

Although only four miles from Stevenage, the village maintains a rural atmosphere. There are a number of farms in the parish, several being in the High Street; Finches Farm that borders the river, and Rooks' Nest Farm whose gracious Elizabethan house has mullioned windows and most distinctive chimneys. Further along the street, at Manor Farm, is a fine 17th-century house and octagonal dovecote, one of the three remaining in the county.

At the northern end of the High Street is the Old Rectory, its pink-washed walls making a perfect setting for the Cedar of Lebanon standing in the foreground. The house was built in 1632 by Daniel Gorsuch for his son John, who became Rector of the church.

By the river in Church End, approached by passing Bridgefoot Farm whose lovely old farmhouse and meadows overlook the ford, stands Hertfordshire's oldest village church, St. Mary the Virgin. Building of the Church commenced some 24 years before the Norman invasion of 1066 and incorporates features from every century since then.

Fairs were held in Walkern in the Middle Ages, festivities being concentrated opposite the White Lion on the King's Highway (now the High Street). From 1880 a fair was held on 5th November each year until 1888 when it was abolished by order of the Secretary of State for the Home Department, owing to rowdy behaviour. Several people living in the village can remember a travelling fair which came to the village green many times during the 1920s and 30s. However, the fair as it is known today was started in 1973 and attracts many people from nearby towns and villages to enjoy the various activities. The event is run by a committee as a charitable concern and benefits various organisations in the village.

Waterford 🦌

To the passing motorist today the village appears to straggle along the A602 for just under half a mile, but this aspect is largely due to the development during the last hundred and twenty years. The main road along the valley of the Beane has been an important highway north from Hertford for many centuries and the hamlet of Waterford grew up near the ford. The latter was needed not for the high road, which continues on the same side of the river, but for a lane turning off to the east.

The first mention of the name Waterford was in the early 13th century. It is thought that the ford may have been so named because the water here was deeper than at Stapleford, a mile and a half upstream. A map printed as late as 1880 still marks the ford, although a bridge was shown as well. Some earlier maps also show bridges but the date when the river was first bridged is not known.

Flimsy constructions would easily have been destroyed in floods such as those that have occurred in living memory.

Today, near the bridge, there are several groups of picturesque old cottages, together with the only remaining public house, The Waterford Arms, and a former hostelry, The Windmill. On the other side of the bridge is a small green. Beside it are two Georgian houses, The Verney, now a residential home for the elderly, and Mill Cottage.

In the late 1860s Robert Smith of Goldings decided to divert the high road from the vicinity of his house. He paid for the construction of nearly a mile of new road which necessitated the building of three new bridges, three culverts and a cutting through Molewood. A new estate road was also built. Such construction work would probably cost well over a million pounds at today's prices. The present main road from the junction with Goldings Lane to Hertford follows the new alignment.

Robert Smith then built a church and put everything of the best of its kind into it. The result is that St. Michael and All Angels is one of the most charming of small Victorian churches. Of particular interest is the stained glass by William Morris Company. The designs were by the different artists who worked for the firm, including Morris himself, Burne-Jones, Ford Madox Brown and Philip Webb. Waterford, previously part of the ancient Bengeo parish became an independent ecclesiastical parish in 1909.

After the consecration of the church in 1872, Robert Smith decided to rebuild Goldings on higher ground, further away from the river mists. This house still stands, a huge neo-Jacobean mansion of red brick. Even his wife noted that it had turned out larger than they would have liked. The family and their descendants lived there for nearly fifty years and then sold it to Dr. Barnardo's.

A great change occurred in April 1922 when the first Barnardo's boys arrived. Two hundred and sixty from Stepney, led by their own band, marched along the road from the railway station at Hertford and took up residence. Later that year the Prince of Wales (later Edward VIII) came for the official opening of the William Baker Technical School as it was called. The large stables of the mansion were ideal for workshops and in the fifty acres of grounds there was plenty of space for a swimming pool and other sports facilities. Two former Barnardo's Boys, Leslie Thomas and Frank Norman have written about their time there in autobiographies. Barnardo's closed the school in 1967 but their apprentice printers continued to live in the Verney for a number of years. Goldings is now used as the headquarters of the Highways Department of the County Council.

Watton-at-Stone

This parish and village is situated five miles north-west from Hertford and twenty-six miles from London. It is supposed to have been formerly the site of a Roman camp and there is reputedly to have been a great battle on this site between the Saxons and the Danes in 1016 and an important chieftain was killed. While they were excavating the Watton-at-Stone bypass site, many Roman remains were uncovered, including over one hundred Roman coins. Many other discoveries were made that have led to the conclusion that Watton was also a market place in Roman times. A Roman road also passed through Watton which started at Verulamium. Another indicator to the age and importance that Watton held in the past is its mention in the Domesday Book and the fact that Watton was part of the manor of Stevenage which was the chief manor of the Abbot of Westminster in the whole of Hertfordshire.

The parish church is dedicated to St. Andrew and St. Mary and is in the Perpendicular style. It contains some impressive stained glass windows and some brasses that date between 1361 and 1614. The parochial registers date from 1560 and are mostly in good condition. During the Civil War, the Roundheads held their royalist prisoners in the church and their graffiti on the walls may still be seen.

From popular belief the village acquired the suffix 'at-Stone' because of two large rocks made of Hertfordshire puddingstone. These were located at the northern end of the village and one can still be seen outside the public house 'The Waggon and Horses'. This enabled the village to be distinguished from the Wattons in Norfolk and Yorkshire. The name Watton appears to have derived from the Saxon word 'Wat' meaning a moist and watery place. Watton has a few natural springs and one of them supposedly had healing properties. At one time Watton was as popular as some of the famous spas like Tunbridge Wells and people came here to take the waters. Unfortunately this particular spring has now dried up.

On the edge of the village, near the railway station, there is a hedgerow which is one of the oldest in Hertfordshire and has many wild plants growing within it. There are many mounds in or around Watton and some are early Roman and Saxon, but many have yet to be excavated. One of the sites has been excavated and it has revealed the ruin of an old church and the remains of a stained-glass window. This window has been proved to be the earliest example of stained glass in Europe.

No village would be complete without a resident ghost and Watton-at-Stone is no exception. A grey lady is supposed to haunt the area around the church twice a year. She is said to haunt this place because she threw herself off the tower after she had been spurned in love.

The village of Watton is now a contrast of old and new and as a result of the increased building and of course an increase in population, the village has had a tremendous achievement because it has succeeded in reversing the current trend of station closures by having its station re-opened after many years, which proves that Watton intends to continue for at least another thousand years.

Welham Green ✤

It could be something in the air, but the skies over Welham Green, North Mymms, seem to hold a fascination for balloonists.

Fortunately for them, the fascination hasn't proved fatal, but it has certainly left its mark on the community.

Near the centre of the village is the spot where Italian balloonist Vincenzo Lunardi touched down in 1784 and put Welham Green on the map forever. His historic flight, the first ballon ascent outside France, gave Welham Green its Balloon Corner and a place in the record books.

Lunardi had set off in his huge red and blue striped balloon from the grounds of the Honourable Artillery Company near Moorfields shortly after 2pm on 15th September. He was watched by an enormous crowd of Londoners, said to have numbered 200,000 and including the Prince of Wales.

For some reason Lunardi took a cat and a dog with him and it was the cat which led to Welham Green's date with destiny. About 90 minutes after his ascent Lunardi paused in the village to let off the airsick animal. The dog, presumably, was made of sterner stuff!

Lunardi's intrepid feat gave its name to one part of the village and in 1960 a commemorative stone was placed at Balloon Corner, at the junction of three roads, Dellsome Lane, Parsonage Lane and Huggins Lane. To do this, part of a corner front garden had to be used. This is mentioned in the deeds of 2 Parsonage Lane, the home of our present publications and press secretary Mrs Dawn Sharpe. Another part of the village – a road of new housing called Vincenzo Close, opposite the shops – also celebrates Lunardi's dramatic stop off.

And bringing the fascinating story up to date, on 15th September, 1984 – 200 years to the day when Lunardi dropped in – villagers again gazed skywards, to watch the ascent of five hot-air balloons, the highlight of a day of fun organised by the parish council to mark this momentous event and the more down-to-earth building of a new sports pavilion.

Welwyn

The river Mimram runs prettily through the village of Welwyn and is bridged in the centre of the main street.

It is quite a common sight to see the traffic come to a halt in order that a line of ducks may cross the road. There is a picturesque access to the river near the bridge and to the north of the village, just after entering Fulling Mill Lane, a pleasant footpath will lead ramblers through the water meadows to the old Welwyn Mill.

Welwyn maintains its fiercely independent identity so that it is not linked or confused with its large modern neighbour, Welwyn Garden City, and its population is swollen by closeness to London and commuterland.

The village has been visited for thousands of years and until 1927 all traffic passed through the village. The road follows an ancient Belgic track, later Roman from St. Albans to Colchester.

There are the village's 'old inns' which can remember coaching days. The Wellington drowses opposite the church and was once a coaching inn known as The Swan. The White Hart was converted from a private house to an inn in 1675. It became one of the principal coaching inns and ran its own coach service to London and could supply changes of horse teams for 80 coaches per day as well as hiring horses and carriages. The White Horse was a public house in 1742, and south of it are a group of cottages locally known as the Assembly Rooms as they were built in 1750 when Dr. Young was promoting the local chalybeate waters as a spa to rival Bath and Tunbridge Wells. Its popularity only lasted 10 years.

Many visitors travelled to Welwyn in those days to visit the house of Dr. Young, the rector, who is little remembered today. In the days of Dr. Johnson and Boswell however, Dr. Edward Young, who was a famous 18th-century poet, had written *Night thoughts on life, death and immortality'*. This obscure tract appealed to the melancholy fashionable in the 1700s when the search for God and truth was thought to be found less in traditional church teaching and more in the beauty of nature. However, Dr. Young must have been ready to take the law into his own hands when he moved from a house in Mill Lane to his new house called Guessens which was further along the road towards Codicote. He realised that he would have to pay a higher coach fare from London, for the fare was charged at the milestone which was always outside the Mill Lane house. The good doctor simply had the milestone pulled up and repositioned hundreds of yards up the road so that his new house was officially still within 25 miles of London.

Close to the village are the arches of the Digswell Viaduct carrying the railway line from London to Scotland. It spans the Mimram valley where Charles Blandis practised his tightrope crossing of the Niagara Falls in 1859, repeating the hair-raising act the following year with a wheelbarrow and a sack.

Another curious Welwyn resident was George Dering of Lockleys, he experimented with wireless before Marconi and also worked on a form of jet propulsion. Dering was eccentric, often disappearing and allowing Lockleys House to fall into neglect. He usually appeared on Christmas mornings to meet the staff of his house then off he would go again. It was only when Dering died that it was learnt that he married under another name and had a separate family in Brighton.

The most important discovery made in Welwyn in more recent years is the Roman Bath House which literally had a motorway built over it. It now lies below the main A1(M) at Welwyn. It was known in 1930 that a Roman villa existed and excavation began. It seems likely the whole site was built about 250 AD. The bath house consists of a hot room, warm room and a cold room. The bather would pass through these rooms graduating from cool to very hot. It was an unhurried process as the baths acted as a social meeting place where the Romans could talk, play energetic games and even listen to poets and musicians as well as eat snack meals.

The Welwyn Bath House was discovered, excavated and saved for the nation by the Welwyn Archaeological Society and is now open to the public at certain times.

West Hyde 🦢

This is the most southerly village in the county and was first mentioned in 796 AD, although there was a settlement there before that date. Flint instruments have been found at nearby Harefield dating from the Stone Age. It has been suggested that the inhabitants were associated with Romans, St. Albans being so close. Pynesfield Manor and five farms were given to the Abbey. Most of south-west Herts at this time belonged to the Abbey.

This has always been a farming community but today only Lynsters Farm is still worked. The land is owned by St. Thomas's Hospital. The farm is mentioned very early in the history of West Hyde and was owned until the 16th century by the Lynsters family. After that the Savoy Hospital owned it then in 1529 all the abbey land was seized and given to St. Thomas's Hospital who have owned it ever since.

Pynesfield Manor is one of the earliest recorded sites in the village dated 796 AD once called Pinnelesfield after the Saxon who lived in the Manor. The name has been changed over the years to Pynesfield. The Lord of the Manor of Rickmansworth owned the Manor in the 17th and 18th centuries. It is said to have the finest small Tudor fireplace in Hertfordshire.

Corner Hall is another house of interest, the style is 18th century and was first owned by the Howard family who also owned Troy Estates, the Troy Estate is now gravel pits. The Bradbery family took over Corner Hall and brought watercress industry to the village. This was a flourishing industry because of the natural springs. H. G. Samson took over the beds in 1926 and farmed them until the early 1960s. The beds have gone and only a stream remains.

May Cottage has its own history, it is 400 years old and was thought to be the original Dower house to Pynesfield Manor. It is timber framed and has an unusual staircase which is square with one continuous newel post to support the treads.

The now demolished Royal Exchange was thought by villagers to be the stables for the King's horses on the royal route to Windsor. In 1817, 29 families lived in the exchange but only 7 houses were built in the mid 1960s on the original site.

The original school house (now privately owned) was built in 1874. In the log books of that time children were absent from school to go gleaning, beating the stag, stone picking, harvesting and wood gathering. Another school was built in 1914 this is now a Youth Centre and H.C.C. Residential Centre. A new school has been built at Maple Cross to cope with the increased population.

Westmill 🦋

It is said that Queen Victoria on her way to visit Lord Hardwicke at Wimpole stopped her carriage on the High Road to admire the village of Westmill. There is no record of her ever coming to visit it which is a great pity for she would have found as so many people do today a beautiful and perfect example of an English Village.

It is situated seven miles from Ware between Puckeridge and Buntingford in a hollow just off the A10 London to Cambridge Road. The river Rib which runs through the recreation ground to the east of the village is at this point a delightful waterway meandering through three-lined banks. At one time a single track railway kept it company running parallel with the Rib for some miles, but no trace of it remains and only the oldest inhabitants remember the little station and mourn its passing.

Because of its small population (there are only about 300 inhabitants) and the layout of the main street and its small green, Westmill has managed to retain the spirit of a village community.

The fine old 11th century Church of St. Mary dominates one end of the street. Made of flint it stands firm, solid and comforting, its clock chiming hourly from the square tower. Its interior, pleasing in its simplicity has one of the tallest Norman arches in the county. Westmill is lucky to have its own rector, and Sunday Services are well attended. The pipe organ is small but a particularly good one. The churchyard is well tended and so peaceful that those visiting there in the spring and summer where there are no noises other than those of nature or the smack of ball against bat from the adjoining cricket field can have little or no doubt that those buried there are indeed at peace. Does the highwayman who was shot and interred there in the year 1800 dream of his nefarious activities on the main road and was he perhaps responsible for the last recorded murder by a highwayman in England. The murder in 1798 of John Mellish M.P. a resident of Westmill.

When stopping for refreshment at the local inn, The Sword in Hand, few people realise it was once the home of a noble Scottish family by the name of Bellenden. It was known at that time as The Old House and the 4th Baron died there of smallpox isolated by his mother in an airless and un-lit attic. Many members of this family are buried in the churchyard. In the year 1800 the house became the inn it is today taking its name from the crest of the Greg family who were at that time squires of the village. The landlord's name at that time was Jackson and the Jackson family remained there for about 150 years.

The miscellany of cottages and houses in the village harmonise well: lath and plaster side by side with flint, feather edged boards near neighbours of brick. A 17th-century house with an adjoining row of 18th-century cottages stand next to the public house whilst opposite the church stand the two oldest cottages in the village built in the 15th century. There are also more fine examples of Georgian houses. A few are thatched, most are tiled but all are a great delight. Where there is modern building it has been carried out discreetly and the small council development blends well.

There are few farm workers these days and those that there are have to be skilled in the use of high powered agricultural equipment and study text books rather than the sky, and yet Westmill is still governed by the farming seasons and folk still talk about 'before hay time' and 'after harvest' their roots still firmly embedded in the soil.

Westmill has a church, a school, a shop and a pub. All the right ingredients to make a happy village, where people with the names of their Westmill ancestors still live, proud of their heritage, where the new mix amicably with the established producing good results, a place to return to, a place to call home.

Weston

JIM WAS BORN IN THIS VILLAGE 1956

The village of Weston sits on top of a hill surrounded by 4 hamlets and 5 towns. It is extraordinary how most of the people in the towns have never heard of us, and yet we overlook them all.

The centre of the village is the Green. The red path across the Green, known as such because of its original red gravel, was made specially for the Manor butler who used to live 't'other side, to save him walking all the way round' so folk say.

The Norman church, Holy Trinity, sits on a hill outside the village with only a few cottages around it. Its isolation is apparently due to the Plague, when the previous surrounding 'village' was destroyed. The grave of Jack o' Legs lies just within the Church gates. He is our legend, a noble highwayman who used to rob the rich and give to the poor.

A factory used to deal with clothing but is now divided into units, one of which makes the Busby hats (bear skin) worn by the Grenadier Guards (outside Buckingham Palace etc.). Weston is the only place where they are made.

Fine housing estates have sprung up in village gaps. Some complained about them when they went up because they didn't look 'villagey', but on the whole they have enhanced the village and brought fresh blood in to stir up, though many a Westonian has remarked that 'we don't know no-one now, when we go up the shop'.

178

Weston boasts a windmill; the sails were taken down in the 1920s for safety. The actual bricks of its construction were made in Weston. There used to be a Tile Kiln as well known to the locals as Ticcal. Two American bombers collided over there during the war and killed a local boy and a mother and baby evacuee.

Wheathampstead

Wheathampstead is a large village which was first recorded as the capital of the Cassivellani, and is now a popular place to live with easy access to M1, A1M and the M25 as well as the London north-eastern and London Midland rail services and Luton airport. Devils Dyke on the eastern boundary of the village is a large earthwork remaining from the days of Cassivellanus. He had his stronghold here against the forces of the Romans under Caesar.

In the 13th century St. Helens church was begun. It is a large flint building with an unusual leaded spire. In the well-designed church there are memorials to much of the village's past. There is a large family memorial for the Cherry-Garrad family, one of whom travelled with Scott to the Antarctic.

Many styles of building are visible in the village centre, the road curving northwards around the octagonal mill house (now a chemists) and mill over the river Lea. Buildings vary in age from the Elizabethan Place Farm to the modern housing recently completed. The baker's shop opposite Place Farm is of wattle and daub construction.

In the early days of the (now removed) railway, laundry was brought from London for washing in the clear country water and air, straw plaits were also made and transported to Luton for the hat industry.

Residents now are mostly people who commute to the large towns nearby or London for work. The village offers a range of varied light industry and the local farming varies from soft fruit through traditional crops and animal husbandry.

The parish of Wheathampstead covers a large area, the nearby town of Harpenden once being part of it. The hamlets of Amwell and Gustard Wood are still in the care of the Parish Council. The Council also looks after a few Harpenden residents whose roads lie within the parish boundary.

The village has its voluntary retained fire brigade as well as many other organisations for the care and well-being of the residents. There are provisions for almost every taste and need, from the babes in arms to the elderly and disabled who have their own club. Wheathampstead is a pleasant place to live with a village atmosphere but a place that also provides a variety of things to give spice to life.

Wigginton 🐿️

In the days when straw plaiting was an important cottage industry, the reputation of Wigginton plaiters was so good that market buyers climbed a steep hill every week to buy their work before it even reached the market!

Wigginton, which appears in the Domesday Book as Wigentone, overlooks the Vale of Aylesbury, nestling on the edge of the Chiltern escarpment. Its presence is not immediately obvious to the busy motorist passing between Tring and Berkhamsted on the A41 but, in recent years particularly, it has become a popular place to live for people seeking the peace of rural life within easy reach of London.

Straw plaiting in Wigginton lasted for just over 100 years, from the beginning of the 19th century until the First World War. Then it was replaced by doll-stuffing and brush making which, in turn, disappeared before the Second World War.

The straw plaiters of the village were mainly the wives and children of men employed by the Rothschild family on their nearby estate at Tring. Many of the houses in the village today were built by the Rothschilds over a period of about ten years at the turn of the century to house the estate workers. Visitors to the village today are always fascinated to see how modern owners have added their own improvements to these houses which are noted locally for their quality and sturdiness. Although originally they were built to just two architectural designs, now no two are alike.

One villager wrote an account of his childhood days during this period when he recalled that Lord Rothschild gave a Christmas hamper to every child in Wigginton and the surrounding villages of St. Leonards, Buckland Common, Cholesbury and Hawridge. The names of every child between the ages of one day and 14 years were taken at the village school in October. On Christmas Eve the hampers, measuring about one foot by two feet, were brought on a covered wagon drawn by four horses with six men to make the deliveries.

As the wagon progressed through the village, it stopped at every house and the hampers, labelled with the name of each child, were left. They contained Christmas sweets, nuts, oranges, two small gifts, a new shilling piece, a 5 lb fruit cake and a box of chocolates. These were the only chocolates most villagers were likely to see in a lifetime.

In years when snow fell, Wigginton boys worried so much about the wagon's arrival that they laid old sacks across the bottom of the hill to make sure it could make the climb!

The recipients of these hampers learned their straw plaiting either at home or at the village plaiting school, opened in the 1870s by a Mrs. Osborne who ran it well into the 20th century. Her son was awarded the Victoria Cross in the Boer War. The school still exists today as a private house, aptly named Osborne Cottage.

Pupils paid one penny a week and received an hour of lessons every day. The rest of the day was spent plaiting, the children providing their own materials. They stayed until the age of 14 when the boys went on the land and the girls returned home to continue their plaiting, thereby contributing valuable extra income at a time when money was scarce.

The plaiters sold their work to the Luton and Dunstable hat makers' agents on Market Day every Friday, making their way to Tring on foot early in the morning. The buying room was in the Rose and Crown – still a prominent landmark in Tring High Street today. As well as selling the finished plaits – a good worker could make about £1 a week when the industry was at its height – the plaiters bought their bunches of straw supplied by the agents for the next week's work. Ideally it was wheat straw about 10 inches long in bundles about 18 inches round.

Once home, the plaiter's first task was to split the straw lengthwise using a cutter or 'cheen' made from tiny brass knives set in wood in a star shape. The resulting strips, called 'splints' were dampened to make them pliable and were then fed through the 'mill' – a small wooden mangle which was sometimes nailed to a door. The arrival of the larger clothes mangle made this job much easier and quicker because of course it took more straw at a time.

Now ready for plaiting, the splints were woven into many designs with such names as whipcord, pearl, bird's eye, plain or brilliant, match box and feather edge. The plaits were either one or two inches wide and once started, would grow rapidly. New splints for 'setting in' were taken with the right hand from a bundle tucked under the left armpit. Women worked indoors or, in finer weather, might gossip by their front doors while plaiting. The work continued when they sat in the garden or walked in the fields, when the growing plait was rolled round the left wrist for ease of carrying.

The final task, usually saved for the Thursday evening before market, was the clipping of the straw ends to make the finished

plaiting tidy – great care was needed not to ruin hours of work by bad cutting!

The plaits were made by the score – 20 yards – and for this purpose most mantelpieces had a yard measure marked on them. Faster workers could do about five yards an hour and an average weekly village output was about 300 score. It was destined for the hat makers of Luton and Dunstable whose influence dominated village life in the rural areas of neighbouring Bedfordshire and Buckinghamshire as well as Hertfordshire at this time.

Now, some seventy years after the disappearance of the industry, village life in Wigginton has changed considerably. The villagers are no longer dependent on the patronage of a landed family for their employment and of course the village has grown in size and numbers. Modern day villagers have, however, managed to retain a strong community spirit. The plaiters' menfolk may have given way to commuters and the like, but still today women gossip on the same doorsteps!

Wilstone 🦢

Undoubtedly the most significant event in the history of the village was the hounding of Ruth Osborn who was branded by local inhabitants as a witch. It was alleged that, after begging for food and being turned away from a farm at Gubblecote, her subsequent mutterings were interpreted as a curse by the farmer. Later events at the farm threw suspicion on Ruth and her husband and a vicious hunt began. Notices were cried at Winslow, Leighton Buzzard and Hemel Hempstead on market days that these two persons would be publicly ducked at Wilstone on 21st April 1751.

When warned by a neighbour, Ruth and her husband took refuge in the workhouse in Tring. The master of this establishment, fearful of the large crowds expected, took the couple and lodged them in the vestry of the church. Great crowds did indeed arrive at the workhouse and so frightened John Thompkins, the master, that he revealed their whereabouts. They were dragged from the church and intervention by the Tring constable, Sebastian Grace, was clearly impossible, for the mob then numbered about

4000. They were repeatedly ducked in a muddy pond at Wilstone, resulting in the death of Ruth who, it was alleged, was held under water by a local chimney sweep named Colley.

Subsequent evidence at the Coroner's inquest held at the Half Moon pub in Wilstone, and later in Tring before the Justices of the Peace of the County, resulted in Colley being lodged in Hertford Gaol where he was hanged on 24th August. As a warning to future offenders his body was brought back to the scene of the crime, accompanied by 108 troopers of the Horse Guards, and hung in chains in Luke's Lane, Gubblecote. Until the wartime airfield at Marsworth necessitated the widening of the lane, many tales were told of strange happenings at this spot, and old Luke was supposed to rattle his chains at late night travellers.

A pond on the outskirts of Wilstone (filled in in recent years) and known as Dinah's pond, was still frightening some villagers until fairly recently. To some people Ruth Osborn was known as Dinah – hence the connection.

Woolmer Green

Woolmer Green has always been divided in two by the road which, more or less, runs through the centre of the community.

How then did the village get its name. On the east side of the main road is a pond or pool, and in 1297 a Thomas de Wolvesmere is thought to have lived in a dwelling nearby. Did he take his name from the 'Wolves Pool' that he lived near? Certainly the area was very thickly wooded at this time and any person living in this area would have used the pool for their water supply. It is thought that several natural springs served the area and this would account for the settlement. A small cul de sac of new dwellings has been given the name of 'Wolvesmere'. In 1984 the pond was cleaned out by a member of the community helped by children from the village. A small island has been established in the centre and a Tortuosa Willow planted. It is stocked with a few carp, is home to various ducks and is once again a focal point for young and old.

Every community has roots and in this respect Woolmer Green does not differ from other rural communities. The roots of

Woolmer Green lie in the Manor lands and many of the cottages in the village have deeds which state that these properties were once part of the Manor of Mardley Bury. This Manor has a long and interesting history which can be traced back to the days before the Norman Conquest. Legend has it that a ghost still haunts this Manor today.

Before 1850 the main occupation of inhabitants was agricultural, but in 1851 the railway had established a line from London to Peterborough which ran through the village on the west side. From that date onwards railway workers became part of the population of Woolmer Green. With the increased population came more building in the village and a school was opened in 1859. A grant of £10 was made by the Great Northern Railway. Money for the building of the school came mostly from donations. Census figures for 1861 show approximately 50 children of possible school age in Woolmer Green. It would appear that all girls up to the age of 13 years are listed as scholars and boys over 10 years are defined as agricultural labourers. The school today, including a nursery class, caters for children between the ages of 3 and 11 years. The building of the school gave the village its first centre for communal activities, there being a small room set aside for religious services. Within this small room began the growth of a religious 'heart' and the villagers became aware of the need for a proper church. This lack of a religious centre could also have been one of the reasons why Woolmer Green remained a backwater for so long.

A Building Fund for Woolmer Green Church was started in the late 1890s. The land upon which the new church was to be built complete with its own churchyard was given by Earl Lytton. The money was raised by voluntary subscription, many people in the area made special gifts towards the 'Ornaments or Furniture' of the church. The foundation stone of the new church was laid by Countess Lytton on 16th September 1899. After a year of hard work and self sacrifice the consecration of the church and burial ground took place on 3rd November 1900, the service being conducted by the Bishop of St. Albans.

Wormley 🦢

Wormley is in the south-east corner of Hertfordshire, and sandwiched between Cheshunt and Broxbourne. It is unusual since it retains the long rectangular shape of a Saxon village, rising from the low-lying river Lee to the high ground bordering the Lee valley, and lies almost due east to west. It is traversed by two major roads, a railway line and a canal, which divide the village into several quite distinct areas. Beside the river Lee is an area of old flood plain and marshland which was once covered by glasshouses and was a major region for the production of salad crops. This trade has become uneconomic in competition with warmer countries and the land is now in the process of development as part of the huge Lee Valley Regional Park which covers some 23 miles from London to Ware. The marshland ends at the London to Cambridge railway line and just over the level crossing is a dense area of housing, some old and newer housing estates with a well-used Community Centre and a separate Over 60s Centre. The older centre of the village is now a Conservation Area cut through by the major road A1170 with a good variety of shops, two Public Houses and nearby is St. Lawrance J.M.I. school. The edge of the conservation area is quite clearly delineated by the New River, which was constructed in 1612 to take pure water from nearby Amwell springs into London. A functional and picturesque piece of engineering which has lasted well through the centuries. Come across the New River into a lane lined with oak trees and an ancient high footpath. On one side is a field with magnificent mature trees and on the other is a huge Recreation Ground with football or cricket pitches according to the seasons. The lane rises steeply to cross over the A10 London to Cambridge road, built in 1973 to bypass Wormley, Broxbourne and Hoddesdon, and continues uphill past the Listed mansion known as Wormleybury with its associated farm buildings and lodges and the sloping meadows of a local farm. At the top of the hill stands Wormley Church, ½ a mile from today's village. It was founded well over 900 years ago and was originally administered by Waltham Abbey. At the extreme western end of the village is a remnant of our Roman history, in the form of a grassy track through woodland, all that is left of the once-busy London to York Roman road called Ermine Street.

186

Wymondley 🦢

The parish of Wymondley lies between the towns of Hitchin, Letchworth and Stevenage. It comprises two ancient villages, Great and Little Wymondley, and also three 'Greens' – Todds Green, Titmore Green and Redcoats Green. Great and Little Wymondley are now one village.

Great Wymondley is still unspoilt – 'Development' not being permitted. Most of it nestles with the Norman Church and Delamere House around a beautiful village green, an ideal setting for the annual village fête. It was here on a sunny June day in 1982 a plaque awarded to The Best Kept Village was presented by Her Majesty the Queen.

In Delamere House, an earlier house than the present, but on the same site, Henry VIII was entertained by Cardinal Wolsey. In the vicinity, immediately south of the church have been found evidence of Roman occupation.

Wymondley Hall and Farm has been the home of the Foster family for several generations. They came to Wymondley first in 1768 from the neighbouring village of Preston. Among their family records is the story of six Foster brothers who assisted John Bunyan while he was in Bedford Jail by taking his place so that he could go out to preach. On one such occasion Bunyan, having a premonition, abruptly broke off his sermon and hurried back to jail just in time to avoid the magistrate who had become aware of these activities.

Just south of the church is moated Wymondley Bury, parts of which date from the 14th century. Some smoke-blackened roof timbers still exist from the days when the smoke from the fires in the great hall went up to the rafters.

Interesting People

Notorious

Walter Clibbon   Datchworth 1782
Footpad. Shot while attacking a local farmer. Buried on Open Valley hill, near Datchworth.

Kathleen Ferrers   Markyate 1650
The wicked lady of Markyate cell – a notorious highway robber.

The Fox twins   Stevenage
Poachers from Stevenage.

Kitt Nash   Tewin
Old Hertfordshire woman poacher, from Harmer Green.

Robert Snooks   Boxmoor
Highwayman. In 1801, robbed a postboy of 6 leather mailbags. He was hanged in 1802.

Dick Turpin
Highwayman.

Jane Wenham   Walkern 17th century
The last woman to be condemned as a witch in England – at Walkern.

Famous/Historical

Harold Abrahams   Great Amwell
The Athlete ('Chariots of Fire').

Alban   St. Albans
First Christian martyr, executed in the city, which now bears his name. Executed *c*209 AD.

Sir Francis Bacon   St Albans
Inherited Gorhambury 1601. Became Lord Chancellor of England. A great lawyer, writer, philosopher and historian.

Sir Albert Barratt   Totteridge
The Sweet Manufacturer.

Lord Bessemer   Hitchin
Inventor. Introduced new steel-making process which bears his name.

General William Booth   Hadley Wood
Came to Hadley Wood in 1889 with his son Bramwell. Founder of the Salvation Army.

Nicholas Breakspear   St. Albans 1155
Born in St. Albans. Enthroned as Pope Adrian IV 1155.

Francis, 3rd Duke of Bridgewater   Berkhamsted
Built the canal of that name. The father of Inland Navigation.

Paul de Caen   St Albans 1077
First Norman Abbott.

Henry Chauncy   Ardeley 1712
Instigated the last witch trial in England in 1712 (Jane Wenham of Walkern). He wrote the first history of Hertfordshire.

Baroness Churchill   Berkhamsted
As Clementine Hozier, lived at 107 High Street.

William Cooper   Berkhamsted
Veterinary Surgeon. 'Coopers Sheep Dip'. Firm now called Wellcome.

Count Esterhazy   Harpenden
Villain of the Dreyfus case. Lived incognito in Harpenden as Count de Villemont.

Celia Fiennes   Great Amwell   1662–1741
Travelled throughout England on horseback and gave eyewitness accounts of the social and economic state of the country.

Viscount Herbert Gladstone   Little Munden   1918–1930
Retired Governor General of South Africa. Son of the Prime Minister Gladstone. Lived at Dane House 1918–1930 approx.

Elizabeth Greenhill   Abbots Langley   17th century
Mothered 32 daughters and 7 sons, all of whom survived to adulthood. Reported in the Guiness Book of Records.

Sir Nigel Gresley   London Colney
Famous Chief Engineer of the L.N.E. Railway.

Nell Gwynn   Shenley
Resided at Salisbury Hall.

The Harmsworth family   Totteridge
Northcliffe newspapers.

Sir John Lawes   Harpenden
Agriculturalist. Founder of Rothamsted Experimental Station. Pioneered the use of artificial fertilizers.

Lord Lister   Hitchin
At school in Hitchin. Inventor of antiseptics.

David Livingstone   Chipping Barnet
Explorer.

Lord Monteagle   Furneux 1605
Received a letter warning him not to attend Parliament on 5th November 1605. Thus the Gunpowder Plot was discovered.

Cecil Rhodes   Bishops Stortford
Founder of Rhodesia.

Baron (John) Somers of Evesham   Welham Green   b1651
Lord Chancellor. Framed the Declaration of Rights. Eased William III and Mary
to the throne.

Dr. Stephenson   Redbourn
Invented writing ink.

Abbott Ulsinus   St. Albans 948 AD
Built St. Peter's, St. Michael's and St. Stephen's churches in St. Albans, thus
defining the city boundaries in 948 AD.

Authors, Actors and Personalities

Gordon Beningfield   London Colney
Naturalist and Painter – attended the local school.

John Betjamen   Chipping Barnet
Poet Laureate.

Barbara Cartland   Essendon
Lives near Essendon.

William Cowper   Berkhamsted   b1731
Poet and Hymn Writer. Father was Rector of Berkhamsted 1722–1756.

E. M. Forster   Stevenage   1879–1970
Childhood spent at 'Rooks Nest', immortalised as Howard's End in his novel of
that name.

Graham Greene   Berkhamsted
Novelist. Father was Headmaster of Berkhamsted Boys School.

Compton McKenzie   Highcross
Lived as a student in Highcross Vicarage.

Henry Moore   Perry Green
Sculptor.

Eric Morecombe   Harpenden
Comedian.

Anna Neagle   St. Albans
Attended St. Albans High School for Girls.

Bernard Shaw   Ayot St. Lawrence
Playwright. Lived at Ayot St. Lawrence 1906–1950.

Ellen Terry   Harpenden
19th century Stage Actress.

E. M. Trevelyan   Berkhamsted
Historian.

H. G. Wells   Digswell
Author. Lived at Digswell.

Barbara Woodhouse   Croxley Green
Animal Trainer, TV personality.

Index